D1561488

Women in Tolstoy

RUTH CREGO BENSON

Women in Tolstoy
The Ideal and the Erotic

UNIVERSITY OF ILLINOIS PRESS
Urbana   Chicago   London

FOR NINA TOLL

Contents

Preface

The conflict between his instincts and his conscience that characterized Tolstoy's entire life was reflected in his double view of woman
as both angel and devil. In his life and in his fiction, Tolstoy believed that women at their best could be loving companions to their
husbands, devoted mothers to their children, and the guardians of
household and family. Woman's selfish interests, however, and particularly her sexuality, constantly threatened Tolstoy's own and his
heroes' search for moral perfection and an ideal of purity. The development of Tolstoy's treatment of this subject in *Family Happiness, War and Peace, Anna Karenina,* and three late short works
gives this study its structure and thematic form. From all of Tolstoy's fiction, these works have been selected because they represent,
in my view, the optimum of thematic relevance and artistic excel-
lence.

Any study of sexuality in Tolstoy must also be, in part, a study of
the related problems in his work of romantic love, marriage, and the
family. In such a study it is traditional for critics to discuss Tolstoy's
personal life, particularly his marriage with Sofiya Andreyevna Bers,
as explanatory background and spiritual stage-setting for his fiction. This approach has been especially true of Tolstoy, in whom the
autobiographer and the novelist are so difficult to distinguish. But,
partly because Tolstoy's life has been so thoroughly discussed, and
partly because of the inherent limits of the biographical in a literary
study, I shall invoke such detail only briefly where appropriate. For
it would be a repetitive exercise in scholarly ingenuity to construct
a concordance of parallels—events, characters, conversations—between the substance of Tolstoy's novels and his own biography. The

references to Tolstoy's personal life will be illuminating, I hope, but they are not intended to be exhaustive.

I have, nevertheless, included in the introductory chapter a brief discussion of Tolstoy's relation to, and memory of, his mother. Her image, I believe, exercised a formative influence on Tolstoy's views of woman as they were reflected in his fiction. It is scarcely possible to examine a writer's relation to his or her mother without immediately suggesting psychoanalytical doctrine and interpretation. My intention, however, is to speak of Tolstoy's image of his mother purely as his model for an ideal type of woman, and thereby to avoid the special pleading of Freudian criticism.

Most Tolstoyan critics have written chiefly about his heroes. This study focuses on the texts most relevant to the study of his heroines. The introductory chapter defines and describes Tolstoy's ambivalent attitudes and feelings toward women. In addition to a brief discussion of *The Cossacks*, Chapter 2 specifically examines Tolstoy's early rejection of romantic love and the possibility of sexual independence for women in *Family Happiness*. Chapter 3 proceeds to a study of Natasha Rostov. Her marriage to Pierre Bezukhov exemplifies Tolstoy's attempt to cope with the destructive force of sexuality by controlling and legitimizing it within the framework of marriage.

Coincidental in Tolstoy's life with his spiritual crisis, *Anna Karenina*, treated in Chapter 4, represents his last comprehensive vision of human relationships. There, radically opposed ideas of woman, love, marriage, and family coexist in equilibrium, if not in resolution. In three late works—*The Kreutzer Sonata*, "The Devil," and "Father Sergius"—this equilibrium collapses into the renunciation of all of the former values and workable institutions most closely identified with Tolstoy's work. I do not, however, conceive of this as a split with Tolstoy's former views, but see it rather as the uncontrolled expression of the nihilism implicit in his earliest work.

In transliterating Russian names in the body of this study I have used System I in J. Thomas Shaw's *The Transliteration of Modern Russian for English-Language Publications* (Madison: University of Wisconsin Press, 1967). For the notes and bibliography, Shaw's System III has been used. Except for Anna Karenina, all feminine endings have been dropped from surnames mentioned in the main discussion.

I wish to thank Alice Pomper for superb assistance in revising and editing the manuscript.

A Note on Documentation and Sources

The Jubilee Edition of Tolstoy (*Polnoe sobranie sočinenij,* Moscow: GIXL, 1928) provided the major source, except where noted, of Tolstoy's diaries, letters, articles, variants to the major works, etc. This edition is referred to as JI (*Jubilejnoe izdanie*) in the text. The commentaries which accompany each issue of this edition were most helpful for background data.

ONE

Introduction: The Divided Image

> "So-called great men are always extremely contradictory.
> . . . But after all, it isn't foolish to contradict yourself: a
> fool may be stubborn, but he never contradicts himself."
>
> Tolstoy in conversation

Possessed of an abundant energy for life and the equally vital power of a hypercritical conscience, Tolstoy lived his life within a self-imposed, frequently self-defeating system of checks and balances. Throughout his entire career he was obsessed with a vision of artistic, intellectual, and moral perfection. In his *Confession* (1879) Tolstoy describes his youth in words that could apply equally well to any period of his life, before or after his struggle to convert from the affluence of a famous aristocrat-author to a life founded on a personal Christianity: "Now, when I think about that time, I see clearly that all the faith I had, the only belief which, apart from mere animal instinct, influenced my life, was a belief in the possibility of perfection, though what it was in itself, or what would be its consequences, I could not have said" (JI 23:4).

The crux of Tolstoy's enigma [1] was his unfortunate capacity to experience life and simultaneously to observe and judge himself in the process. Though beneficial or perhaps even necessary in a great writer, this incessant *voyeurism* led Tolstoy to deprecate and reject his intellectual, artistic, moral, and cultural life and, at the same

---

1. The title of a critical study by M. Aldanov (pseud. Landau), *Zagadka Tolstogo* (Berlin: I. P. Ladyžnikov, 1923). This book and an article by Renato Poggioli (see note 2) examine the question of Tolstoy's "split."

time, to condemn his failure to achieve a higher standard of perfection. The guilt and self-reproach which inevitably accompanied these "failures" were heightened by his pervasive self-consciousness, his "tragic sincerity," [2] and a conscience of such proportions that he was once humiliated at trying but not succeeding to love rats.[3]

Tolstoy's conversion to what he conceived to be the peasant virtues of selflessness, simplicity, resignation, and belief began and matured in the mid- to late 1870s. During that period he confronted the inevitability and the finality of death, central to his spiritual crisis, with the question "Why?" Why, Tolstoy asked, did he want wealth, power, and fame? Why had he written books like *War and Peace* and *Anna Karenina?* Why did white-gloved servants serve at his table? Why was he married and bringing up children? But this moral crisis of the 1870s was not unique to the dialectic of his life and thought. Although the term is more often associated with Dostoevsky, it accurately describes the process of quest, solution, disillusion, and reorganization that characterized Tolstoy's life and work of eighty-two years.

The problem of sexuality was crucial to the cleavage existing between Tolstoy's deepest instincts and the moral superstructure by which he judged them. From his youth to his old age, Tolstoy was body-haunted, obsessed equally by sexual desire and the guilt of sexual satisfaction. In the diary of his youth he claims that "I'm dissatisfied with only one thing: I cannot overcome my sensuality, especially because it is a passion which has now become a habit with me" (JI 46: 37). Although he defined the moral dimensions of sexuality in the traditional terms of the mind-body problem, he occasionally envisioned the happy integration of flesh and spirit as, for example, when he claimed that "the objective of the spirit is the good of one's neighbor, but the objective of the flesh is one's

2. Renato Poggioli, "A Portrait of Tolstoy as Alceste," in *The Phoenix and the Spider* (Cambridge, Mass.: Harvard University Press, 1957).
3. Aldanov, *Zagadka Tolstogo,* p. 118.

own personal good. In the mysterious bond between the soul and the body lies the solution of conflicting aims" (JI 46: 140). Another entry in his diary of that period describes his own sexual impulses as natural; they "seem bad" only because of his "unnatural" position as a bachelor (JI 46: 94).

Yet these are isolated passages. The preponderant number and the violent tone of most of Tolstoy's remarks on sex amply testify to his most basic feelings. He felt that men in the pursuit of a rationally conceived and morally dedicated life are torn by the contradictory convictions of the spirit and the desires of the flesh: "The flesh should be a well-trained dog to the soul, going wherever the soul sends it. And look at us! The flesh is riotous and indefatigable, and the soul follows it in pathetic helplessness." [4] Men are, consequently, vulnerable to temptation, in constant danger of capitulating to their lowest instincts, as he once defined them: "Everyone knows and agrees that sexual relations debilitate and exhaust a person, debilitate him precisely in the most essentially human function, the function of the intellect." [5] In this view Tolstoy reflected both his period and his class.

In his diary of 1851, Tolstoy describes the following episode:

I couldn't resist signalling to someone in a pink dress who, from a distance, looked very attractive to me, and I opened the door behind me. She entered. I couldn't even see her; it all seemed foul and repulsive, and I actually hated her for having made me break my rule. In general it is a feeling which very much resembles the hatred you feel toward people to whom you can't explain that you don't like them, but who have the right to think that you do like them. A sense of duty, a sense of disgust—both spoke against it. [JI 46: 59]

4. M. Gor'kij, *Lev Tolstoj; Sobranie sočinenija* (Moscow, 1951), vol. 14, p. 298.

5. Quoted in L. Tolstoi, *Church and State and Other Essays* (Boston, 1891), p. 163.

The humiliation over his vulnerability was quite naturally reflected in Tolstoy's feelings about women. Since, according to him, they both provoked and were the object of sexual activity, women became the scapegoats for the self-reproach, the guilt, and the self-hatred that inevitably followed Tolstoy's sexual indulgence. Tolstoy once said to his friend Goldenveizer that "women are generally so bad that the difference between a good and a bad woman scarcely exists." [6] But Tolstoy's feelings and attitudes toward women were obviously divided, for he created not only coarse, cruel women like Ellen Kuragin, but such attractive figures as Natasha Rostov, who equals Pushkin's Tatyana as a nationally revered literary heroine. These contradictory images of unique but stereotypical women were drawn from various sources in Tolstoy's life and imagination.

After the age of seven, when his father died, and all during adolescence, Tolstoy was surrounded and cared for almost exclusively by women. And as an old man, when he was dying at Astapovo, he was once again surrounded by the women of his own family—allied with his daughters, alienated from his wife. The impact of both his happiness and his long conflict with his wife, Sonya, on his life and work cannot be denied or ignored. But Tolstoy's idealized image of his mother, not so often discussed as his relations with his wife, is certainly as important, for his ideal literary heroines are modeled in part upon that image.

For Tolstoy, there was no woman more sacred than his mother, Marya Nikolayevna. Although she died when he was only a year and a half old, the image he formed of her, through a few mementoes and the reminiscences of other relatives, was extraordinarily vivid and penetrated his imagination until the day he died. Her fictional counterpart occupies a prominent place in his letters, memoirs, and novels. His portrait of Nikolay's mother in

6. A. B. Gol'denvejzer, *Vblizi Tolstogo* (Moscow: GIXL, 1959), p. 51.

Childhood is close in tone and feeling to his nonfictional reminiscences of his own mother:

> So many past memories arise when one tries to recall the features of
> a beloved being, that one sees those features dimly through the
> memories as if through tears. They are the tears of imagination.
> When I try to recall my mother as she was at that time I can only
> picture her brown eyes, always expressing the same kindness and
> love, the mole on her neck just below the place where the short hairs
> curled, her embroidered white collar, and the delicate dry hand
> which so often caressed me and which I so often kissed, but her
> general expression escapes me. [JI 1: 8]

An entry in his diary written almost half a century after he completed *Childhood* testifies to the endurance of these sentiments:
"If I could only be little again and snuggle up to my mother as I
imagine her to myself! Yes, yes; the mother whom I called to when
I could not speak, my highest image of pure love; not cold, divine
love, but earthly, warm, motherly. That is what my battered, weary
soul is longing for." [7] Another entry of that same period reveals
that his mother "remained for [him] a holy ideal" (JI 56: 133).

When he wrote his *Recollections,* Tolstoy described how his
mother spent her time: "My mother's life was spent in the care of
her children, reading novels aloud to my grandmother in the evening, in serious reading such as Rousseau's *Emile,* in discussing
what had been read, in playing the piano, in teaching Italian to
one of my aunts, in walks and in managing the household"
(JI 34: 354). Among her few souveniers Marya Nikolayevna left two
poems which reveal other aspects of her elusive life and character.
These poems have a selfless, gentle quality and project a sentimental
notion of her marriage. Beyond that, they reveal a conventional
woman of the period who, accepting her marital fate with gratitude

7. *Dnevnik* (1900), quoted in Janko Lavrin, *Tolstoy: An Approach* (New
York: Macmillan, 1946), p. 18. The *Dnevnik* of 1900 (JI 54), however, does
not contain this passage.

and finality, asks only that her husband be, in the words of one of
the poems, "as happy as he is loved." [8]

This ultradomestic image of his mother influenced and reinforced
Tolstoy's demanding and limited standard for the "ideal" woman.
In his strictly traditional view, he pictured her as a loving and
submissive wife, a gentle and dedicated mother, and a warm and
loyal supporter. This notion changed little over the years and is
entirely consistent in tone with a late statement (1895) concerning
women which appeared in Tolstoy's *Krug Chteniya* as an appendix
to Chekhov's story *Dushechka:* "Without mothers, helpers, friends,
comforters who love in a man all that is best in him, and who, with
barely noticeable suggestions, inspire and support all the best in him
—without such women it would be difficult to live in this world"
(JI 41 : 376).

It is evident from the *Recollections* that Tolstoy believed his
mother to be "morally superior to [his] father and his family, with
the exception of Tatyana Alexandrovna Ergolsky, with whom [he]
lived half [his] life and who was a woman of remarkable moral
qualities." [9] Tatyana Ergolsky, a distant relative of Tolstoy's father
and the ward of his grandmother, cared for the Tolstoy children
after their mother's death. He describes her in his recollections as
the person who influenced his life the most. She loved Tolstoy very
much and he reciprocated that love as to a real mother: "I had fits
of rapturously tender love for her. I remember that once when I
was about five, I squeezed in behind her on the sofa in the drawing
room, and how, caressing me, she touched my hand. I caught her
hand and began to kiss it and cry from tender love of her" (JI 34:
365). In fact he claims that her influence on his life "consisted first
of all in teaching me from childhood the spiritual delight of love.

8. S. Tolstoj, *Mat' i ded L. N. Tolstogo* (Moscow, 1928), p. 110.
9. JI 34: 350. Tolstoy's remarks on his mother, pp. 349–54; on his aunt, pp.
364–70.

She did not teach me that by words, but she filled me with love by
virtue of her whole being" (JI 34: 366–67).

But Tolstoy was not completely happy with the source of that
love. He complains that her chief characteristic was love—"but
. . . much as I wished that it were different, it was love for one
man, my father. Only from that center did her love radiate to everyone. We felt that she loved for his sake. Through him she loved
everyone, for her whole life was made up of love" (JI 34: 366).

Tolstoy wrote in some detail about his father, Nikolay Ilyich,
in his *Recollections,* drawing there a congenial country squire, a
loving and beloved father, who was in no way extraordinary—
rather like Nikolay Rostov of *War and Peace.* The following
passage from his portrait is typical:

> But I understood then that my father never humbled himself before
> anyone and never changed his debonair, gay, and often ironic tone.
> And this sense of personal dignity which I noticed in him increased
> my love for and my delight in him.
>
> I remember his merry jests and stories at dinner and supper, and
> how grandmother and my aunts and we children laughed, listening
> to him. I also remember his trips to town, and how wonderfully
> handsome he looked when he wore his frockcoat and narrow trou-
> sers. [JI 34: 357]

Most of Tolstoy's recollective descriptions of his family are in
tone and style characteristic of the genre; they are charming and
often gently ironic portraits. But in his image of his mother there is
something different: that unblemished picture of his mother as a
saintly woman which he retained throughout his life is one aspect
of his search for "the ideal" and for unchanging truth which would
give life form and meaning. She is frequently referred to in religious
terms, as when Tolstoy wrote late in life that his mother had remained for him "a holy ideal." He mentions in the *Recollections*
that he prayed to her spirit: "When I was struggling with over-

whelming temptations, I prayed to her spirit, begging her to aid me, and those prayers always helped me" (JI 34: 354). In *Childhood* there is an even stronger suggestion of the identity of the image of mother with God: "When I repeated the prayers which my baby lips had first lisped along with my beloved mother, my love for her and my love for God mingled strangely into one feeling" (JI 1: 44).

Because Tolstoy hardly knew his mother and because she left very little that reveals more of her nature, it was very hard for him to know what kind of person she really was. That no picture of his mother survived indeed helped Tolstoy the more easily to think of her as perfect: "I don't remember my mother at all. I was one and one half years old when she died. It somehow happened that not a single portrait of her remained; so that I can't picture her as a physical being. In a way, I'm glad for that, because in my concept of her there is only her spiritual image and everything that I knew about her is wonderful . . ." (JI 34: 349). Thus his idea of her was safe, unchallenged even by a photograph. But, both consciously and unconsciously, Tolstoy did compare the women he personally encountered with this icon of ideal womanhood. In fact he once wrote: "Everything I've loved—a dog, a horse, a woman—I've always compared with an ideal of perfection for that particular species." [10] And that "ideal of perfection" for the species "woman" was modeled upon his mother. In *Anna Karenina*, the intensity of that image is purely reflected in Levin's dream of a family life patterned after that of his own parents': "Levin scarcely remembered his mother. The thought of her was sacred to him and in his imagination his future wife was to be a repetition of that enchanting and sacred ideal of womanhood which his mother had been" (JI 18: 101).

Yet the purity of the image of woman modeled upon Tolstoy's memories and fantasies of his own mother only perpetuated and

10. Quoted in E. Simmons, *Leo Tolstoy* (Boston, 1946), p. 142.

intensified the inevitable conflict with his view of woman in reality as egocentric, emotionally erratic creatures, whose erotic influence was a constant threat to man's best impulses. (Wasn't it true, after all, that his aunt's love for him had its source in her sexual love for his father?) This rule for conduct recorded in Tolstoy's early diary sums up concisely his general attitude—which continued until his death:

> Regard the society of women as an inevitable evil of social life, and avoid them as much as possible. Because from whom do we actually learn voluptuousness, effeminacy, frivolity in everything and a multitude of other vices, if not from women? Who is responsible for the fact that we lose such feelings inherent in us as courage, firmness, prudence, equity, and so on, if not women? Women are more receptive than men, and during the age of virtue were better than we were; but now in this age of corruption and vice they are worse than we are. [JI 46: 32–33]

It was this view of woman which led Tolstoy to declare that woman is "in all respects, morally [man's] inferior" [11] and which was the source of that "implacable hostility" toward her which Gorky observed.[12]

In conversation Tolstoy once said that he was "still going to write someday about women—when I'm very old and have stomach trouble, and when I look at the world out of the corner of my eye. Then I'll stick my head out and tell them: There! That's what you're like—and then scram as fast as I can. Or else they would peck me to death." [13] In any examination of Tolstoy's writing about women before this imaginary venture, it is impossible to avoid the immediate impression that they—and, indeed, his deepest feelings about them—are extremely ambivalent. A detailed scrutiny reveals

11. D. Merejkowski, *Tolstoi as Man and Artist* (New York and London: G. P. Putnam and Sons, 1902), note 51.

12. Gorkij, *Lev Tolstoj,* p. 265.

13. Gol'denvejzer, *Vblizi Tolstogo,* p. 55.

not merely the existence of contradictory attitudes toward women, but a radical tension between polarized attitudes toward women and a capacity to think of them only in extreme terms. In sum, Tolstoy fully subscribed to the orthodox Western view.

This divided image of woman is illustrated nicely in a late journal entry in 1898. He stated there that "all the women of our Christian world" are "impure." But, he continued, "all this concerns women who are not Christians, impure women, like all the women of our Christian world. Oh, how I would like to show to women all the significance of a chaste woman. A chaste woman . . . will save the world" (JI 53:210). A few days later he added: "One of the most necessary tasks of humanity consists in the education of a chaste woman" (JI 53:208).

In these assertions Tolstoy expressed his personal horror at the immorality of the real women in the society around him, and his lopsided vision of the absolute importance of chastity in the ideal woman. Yet these statements were made near the end of his life, and they are the outraged protests of a man who had lost hope of finding any goodness in the world, in conventional morality or institutions. The ideal is depicted in these remarks as unattainable and infinitely remote from the real world. They are, in short, statements expressing the feelings and attitudes fictionally reflected in *The Kreutzer Sonata,* and they indicate the late Tolstoy's severely radicalized view of women. This reaction was not a reversal of his early views; it is a caricature, a grotesque exaggeration of them.

Both of Tolstoy's icons of woman—as devil and as angel—have one thing in common: they completely reject sexuality. To displace the body from the center of her universe and therefore from the center of *man's* universe is Tolstoy's basic demand of woman. For he thought of women—"real women"—as either sexual agents or sexual objects. Vladimir Chertkov, Tolstoy's friend and disciple, assures us that though there may be evidence of hostility toward women in Tolstoy's work and thought, "he absolutely discriminated in favor of the intelligent, religious woman whom he seldom happened to meet in life and who always attracted his attention."[14] Tolstoy's "best" women in this sense are bodiless, deprived of all passions save those directed toward family, chastity, or the Christian ideals of self-effacement and asceticism.

Tolstoy's assumption that women used sexuality either as an end in itself or to secure selfish wishes reflects his general skepticism about their rationality and morality. Repeating again and again that they are ruled by their emotions, not by their thoughts, he shared the traditional belief that women are basically irrational and immoral. He once wrote about his conflict with his own wife, that "it is impossible to predict what will happen. With us men, thought influences action. But with women, especially feminine women, actions influence thought . . ." (JI 73–74: 57). When Tolstoy encountered the products of women's intellectual efforts, he distrusted them. Commenting on Catherine II's *Nakaz,* a 1766 treatise on civil rights, the young Tolstoy observed that it was the "fruit of a woman's intellect, which for all its acumen could not suppress the petty vanity which obscures its high merits" (JI 46: 27). As for woman's moral capacity: "It is impossible to demand from a woman that she evaluate . . . her love on the basis of moral feeling. She cannot do it because she does not possess real moral feeling, that is, one that overrides everything" (JI 53: 209).

Conceiving of women thus, as creatures absolutely deprived of both intellectual and moral capacity, Tolstoy believed them to be primarily motivated by an egocentric and devilish self-interest. *All* of their activity, he believed, was primarily and even exclusively directed toward themselves. It is true that this view was most strongly expressed toward the end of his life, particularly in the

14. V. Chertkov, Afterword to *The Journal of Leo Tolstoy 1895–1899,* tr. R. Strunsky (New York, 1917), pp. 337–39.

1890s. But even in the 1860s, when *War and Peace* was begun, his response was much the same.

His attitude toward the "woman question" is a case in point. Socially conscious Russians of the mid-nineteenth century were focusing much of their thinking and writing on the status of women. For the first time the possibility of political and social privileges and responsibilities for women, including university and professional training, was given serious if not extensive consideration. For the first time, "progressive" women and men, influenced by such social critics as Chernyshevsky, were deeply concerned with women's chance to take full part in Russian life.[15]

But Tolstoy, whose "ideal woman . . . bears children and raises them as Christians" (JI 54:22), despised the movement for women's emancipation, even its most conservative demands. His play *The Infected Family*, begun in 1836, is an acid caricature of the feminist movement. His portrait of its short-haired heroine, Katerina Dudkina, is venomous; he refuses to treat her as a serious person with serious ideas. Other heroines either ignore feminist aspirations, like Natasha Rostov, or like Anna Karenina, experience the disastrous consequences of achieving them, however narrowly defined.

On this issue Tolstoy's casual comments were as revealing as the more formal, polemical aspect of his fiction. Goldenveizer's memoirs yield this characteristic remark of Tolstoy on the subject: "If I were a minister, I should issue an edict which would require all women to enter universities and which would deprive them of the right to marry and have children. For the infringement of this law, the guilty would be liable to a heavy penalty. Then they would all be

15. I. S. Turgenev's *Ocy i deti* (1855), *Rudin* (1856), and *Asja* (1858), and N. G. Černyševskij's *Čto delat'* (1864) typify, among other works, the literature most representative of and sympathetic to the "woman question" of the 1860s and its allied sociopolitical issues. For a concise and acute discussion of this in relation to Tolstoy, see B. M. Ejxenbaum, *Lev Tolstoj* (Leningrad: 1928), vol. 3, pp. 131 ff.

sure to marry!"[16] The marriage of his daughter Tanya in 1898 prompted the following entry in his diary: "For seventy years my opinion about women has fallen lower and lower, and it's still falling even lower. The woman question! How can there not be a woman question? But it should have nothing to do with how women should begin to direct life, but how they should stop ruining it" (JI 53: 231).

Tolstoy believed that woman's place is in the home. She should love and care for her husband and perhaps even more devotedly for her children: "The confused modern idea is that a woman's capacity to give herself up with all her being to love is obsolete and dead; and yet this is her most precious, her best quality, and it is her true vocation—not political meetings, academic courses, revolutions, etc."[17] His most specific statement on this appears in a brief posthumous fragment entitled "On Marriage and the Vocation of Women," according to which woman should dedicate herself entirely to the physical and spiritual welfare of the family—for she is biologically and emotionally marked for this role. She should ideally abstain from all outside interests, most particularly social activities and fashion, intellectual interests, and political action (JI 7: 133–35). One critic sums up this insistence on domesticity very neatly:

> When we look at the female types introduced in Tolstoy's works, we should first of all notice the narrowness of their portrayal: the women are presented by the author exclusively from the physiological side; "woman-mother," "woman, female-of-the-species"—that is his ideal; he looks negatively upon the "woman question"; he values the duty of the mother and in elemental motherhood sees the guarantee of highest ethical perfection; child-bearing is the duty of woman and her sole service to humanity.[18]

16. Gol'denvejzer, *Vblizi Tolstogo,* p. 157.
17. *Ibid.,* p. 159.
18. N. Trubicyn, *Obščestvennaya rol' ženščiny v izobraženii novejšej russkoj literatury* (Moscow: M. & S. Sabašnikov, 1907), pp. 15–16.

In his apotheosis of marriage and family life, Tolstoy accepted the conventional view that marriage was an institution whose primary function was to control an otherwise chaotic and unhealthy sexuality—for man and for woman—and to promote a microcosmic, civilized order in the family. Even in his mature years, when fear of and hostility toward women had already become a dominant theme in his thought and writings, he was still capable of representing fictionally such nearly ideal relationships as that of Natasha and Pierre, or Kitty and Levin, whose marriages embodied this vision. In his twenties, his personal expectations of love and marriage were as idealistic as his portrayals of those two relationships. A simple and eloquent expression of his early attitudes appears in this letter to his aunt: "I am thinking of the happiness awaiting me. . . . This is a wonderful dream. But this is not all that I allow myself to dream of. I am married; I have a kind, quiet, loving wife: she loves me as much as I love her, we have children who call you "grandmother" (JI 59: 160).

Marital intercourse (as opposed to random coupling), sanctioned by law and a higher moral order, was in this conception a creative act whose end was the expansion and continuation of life. By incorporating sexuality into a larger scheme of biological and moral order, Tolstoy, at least until the later period of his life, attempted to remove its stigma and legitimize its force. Yet the potential failure of marital discipline continued to threaten Tolstoy's vision, and moved him to try to deny the romantic core of marriage. In his *Recollections* he writes of his own parents' marriage that "my mother's very short married life—hardly more than nine years— was a good and happy one. It was a very full one and adorned by her love of all who lived with her and by everybody's love of her. . . . I think that my mother was not in love with my father, but loved him as a husband and chiefly as the father of her children" (JI 34: 352).

This is suggestive of Tolstoy's early distinction between a happy marriage and romantic love. Because romantic passion, as he conceived it, is essentially self-serving and therefore limiting, Tolstoy found it debasing, unworthy, and destructive of domestic harmony. So that for all his desire to fall in love and be loved in return, Tolstoy could write, in a plan for a projected novel, that "love does not exist. There exists the physical need for intercourse, and the rational need for a mate in life" (JI 46: 146). Renato Poggioli confirms and enlarges on this view when he argues that

> Eros, as distinguished from sex, played a small role in his biography, and even less in his works. . . . Tolstoy as a man was successively attracted by three different tendencies, promiscuity, uxoriousness, and asceticism, each one of which in its special way is a denial of romantic love. While *l'amour-passion* derives from a profane apotheosis of the Eternal Feminine, promiscuity, uxoriousness, and asceticism are but different forms of the same contempt for woman. In brief, Tolstoy was not only, like Alceste, a misanthrope: unlike him, he was a misogynist too.[19]

Tolstoy hoped to encounter in life, or failing that, create in his fiction women who embodied his heightened conception of them as devoted wives and mothers living in harmony with their roles determined by nature. Their potential to sexually seduce and morally degrade men would thus be neutralized. This enticing ideal, however, could not resist Tolstoy's power as a writer. For, except in such one-dimensional heroines as Maryanka (*The Cossacks*) or Pashenka Mikhailovna ("Father Sergius"), his ideal woman could never materialize in his kind of fiction. The more complex heroines of his fiction were treated with the same ambivalence which he felt toward women in actual life. It provides, in fact, the vitality and the humanity of his greatest heroines. Though this ambivalence is not always readily apparent, it is nonetheless present and formative throughout his writing.

19. Poggioli, *The Phoenix and the Spider*, p. 70. (When women become people, such semantic turns many well disappear!)

TWO

Early Portraits of Romantic Love

Romanticism is the fear of facing the truth.

Tolstoy in conversation

I

Of Tolstoy's early works, *The Cossacks* and Part I of *Family Happiness* share an unflawed vision of an ideal love relationship. Although *The Cossacks* was published in 1862, Tolstoy had begun work on it ten years earlier when he himself, at that time a soldier in the Caucasus, was immersed in the life it describes. During the decade between the inception and completion of *The Cossacks, Family Happiness* was conceived, written, and published. In his discussion of *Family Happiness*, Eikhenbaum describes its appearance as a "sudden" and "abrupt" phenomenon within that decade.[1] Yet the original plan for *The Cossacks*, cited by Eikhenbaum himself, shows not only a direct connection with *Family Happiness*, but with the development of Tolstoy's fictional themes in general.

Tolstoy originally intended *The Cossacks* to be a three-part novel. The first became *The Cossacks* as we know it today—the story of a young officer, Olenin, who in the Caucasus falls in love with a Cossack girl, Maryanka, but eventually returns to his former life. In the projected second part of the novel, however, Maryanka and her betrothed, Lukashka, marry; Olenin renews his pursuit of her, but leaves with Lukashka to fight in the mountains. In the final part, Olenin, in the village once again, finally wins Maryanka, they live

1. Ejxenbaum, *Lev Tolstoj*, vol. 1, p. 344; general discussion of *Family Happiness* in vol. 1, pp. 344–71.

together, but their relations become increasingly disappointing. Lukashka returns and is executed, and Olenin is murdered either by a rival or Maryanka.[2]

In view of this plan, it is safe to suggest that *Family Happiness* was not a hastily executed literary venture but rather one which isolated and explored a theme from the projected third part of *The Cossacks*. The heroine of *Family Happiness* is, like Olenin, moved by the romantic impulse toward pure love and moral perfection. But once married, her romantic illusions are destroyed and eventually transformed into a subdued, chastened adaptation to domestic reality. The themes of moral retribution and homicidal jealousy, also present in the original plan for *The Cossacks,* were of course fully elaborated in *Anna Karenina* and *The Kreutzer Sonata. The Cossacks,* as it is briefly discussed in this chapter, will be considered complete. For it represents in any case a unique attempt in Tolstoy to legitimize the sexual relationship of man and woman by associating it with nature and the "natural ideal." By itself, *The Cossacks* remains, in fact, so pure, stark, and finally unreal, that it strays from the conventions of the short story into the abstract world of myth.

The Cossacks as published tells the story of Dmitry Olenin, a young aristocrat of the 1840s, who flees from gambling debts and an impossible love affair in Moscow to the Cossack village of Novomlinsk in the Caucasus. Though autobiographical, *The Cossacks* portrays the young soldier Tolstoy would have liked to have been in the mountains instead of the one who actually lived there in the early 1850s. For Tolstoy's way of life there continued and exacerbated the chronic state of self-dissatisfaction and desire for self-improvement which one can see in his personal diaries of those years. The diaries record feelings and events very different from the ascetic life of Tolstoy's fictional counterpart. In the Caucasus, Tolstoy indulged in every "vice" he had wanted to escape. He partied with the gypsies and Cossack women, he gambled and drank:

2. For variants, see JI 6.

July 3. I wrote the above on June 13th, and have wholly wasted my
time because on the same day I got so carried away that I lost at
cards 200 rubles of my own money, 150 of Nikolenka's, and got
into debt for 500—total 850. However, I am keeping myself in hand,
and living prudently. I rode over to Chervlenaya and got drunk
there. [JI 46: 64–65]

Far from leaving Moscow and its temptations, as Olenin did, Tolstoy took Moscow to the Caucasus.

In *The Cossacks,* Olenin thinks with humiliation of the kind of
life he and his friends had been living in Moscow. Without moral
or emotional responsibilities, as "only a Russian of the 1840s can
be" (JI 6:7), he has contracted the usual heavy debts at fashionable
restaurants, at his French tailor, and at cards. To Olenin, all these
are merely the concrete expression of the idle and wasteful nature of
his life. Like Masha in *Family Happiness,* he feels all the super-
abundant energy of youth, but has no focus for it. Like the head-
waiter in a restaurant which he frequents, his society places high
value on position and rank. Olenin too, half-consciously and "despite himself," is drawn to the same superficial judgments.

He has enthusiasms, but they are ephemeral, and he is skeptical
and suspicious of them. They are comfortable and acceptable only
insofar as they leave him free: "As soon as he felt that one of his
interests would require work and effort, he instinctively disengaged
himself from the feeling or the pursuit and regained his freedom.
This is how he approached society, work, the management of his
estate, music . . . and also love for women, which he did not believe in" (JI 6:8). Olenin's concept of freedom is significant: it is
the intentional cultivation of total noncommitment. And everything
for which he criticizes society—vanity, idleness, extravagance—is
rooted in this disengagement. Every criticism he makes of his society is a self-indictment; he himself reflects, embodies, and perpetu-
ates its follies and failings.

His journey to the Causasus, Olenin hopes, will yield self-discovery and redemption: "he was making a new start, and from then on there would be no mistakes, no regrets, nothing but certain happiness" (JI 6:8). Olenin has hypnotized himself with the myth of the "fresh start"—the possibility that he will be different and better in another environment. In this hope rested Tolstoy's own dream of perfection, that search for an ideal truth which haunted him all his life and which no actual event or relationship could ever match.

An important part of Olenin's vision of his future was the possibility of falling in love. In Moscow, he had wondered if he were a "moral aberration," since he had so far found no one to love. Whenever he seemed to be on the brink of love, he suddenly felt that this was "not it" (JI 6:9). He would be seized with passion at a ball but would wake up the next morning to find that love had vanished. Curiously unaware that his habit of emotional disengagement could seriously affect the lasting quality of these *grands passions,* Olenin utterly fails to distinguish between love and passing fancy.

In his fantasy of future romance, he is blissfully unconscious of such problems. His dreams reveal a long-haired Caucasian girl with "deeply humble eyes" waiting at the door to greet her hero returned from the wars. Though her "wild, primitive ignorance" delights him, he begins to educate her (JI 6:11). So quick and talented is she, that, as Olenin's fantasy boils over, she begins to speak French, sing, run a *salon*—in a word, she becomes the kind of woman he has found so trivial and unacceptable in the past.

When Olenin at last arrives at the Cossack village of Novomlinsk, he enters a masculine society whose interests and values differ vastly from Moscow's. Olenin has quickly perceived that the Cossack men are in nature and of nature: their total ethic derives from this source. Their primary concern is survival, and warfare is their mode of life. Death—one's own or another's—is a natural event to be resolutely accepted without melodrama, not a philosophical problem to ponder or fear. This attitude makes courage and cunning unsentimentally prized qualities: they are equally important not only for warfare and survival, but also for drinking and horsestealing. The measure of a man is simple—how much *chikhir* can he drink, how many woman does he have, and how many enemies has he killed?

Somewhat to Olenin's chagrin, the purpose of Cossack life seems to be glory and good times. A man is loved and rewarded if he has killed an enemy or if he can drink a lot. Part of this freewheeling ethic is its liberal sexual code. Since free exchange of partners prevails, and married and betrothed men and women are free to substitute and supplement their intended partners, chastity is a novel and naive condition. On announcing that it would be sinful for the old man to procure for him a Cossack woman, Olenin receives the following advice from Uncle Yeroshka, his wise old Cossack friend: "Sinful? What's sinful? You think it's a sin to look at a beautiful girl? Is it sinful to love her up a little? Maybe where you come from it's a sin. No sir, brother, it's no sin—it's salvation. God made you and he made the girl, he made everything. So, it's no sin to look at a pretty girl; she's made to be loved and to make us happy. That's the way I figure it, friend" (JI 6:47). In a moment of balance on the sexual question, Tolstoy much later in life echoed this sentiment: "If a girl is over fifteen and healthy, she likes to be embraced and touched. Her mind is fearful of what is unknown and of what she does not yet understand—that is what is called modesty. . . . But her body is already aware that the unknown is inevitable and legitimate, and, despite the mind, demands the fulfillment of its law." [3] In spite of Uncle Yeroshka's advice, Olenin is appalled at fellow officers like Beletsky who are capable of throwing themselves into the life of the community, especially its sexual life. Olenin finds it difficult to grasp how "the Cossacks, able to assess Beletsky clearly as a man who likes his wine and his women, grew accustomed to him

3. Gorkij, *Lev Tolstoj,* pp. 291–92.

and preferred him to Olenin, who remained a mystery to them" (JI 6:90).

Yet the wild beauty and natural charm of his landlord's daughter, Maryanka, dispels Olenin's ascetic notions, and he falls in love with her. Though Maryanka is the embodiment of his primitive dream-girl, her love for and formal betrothal to Lukashka provides a "barrier" between her and Olenin. But she darts in and out of his sight and thoughts, constantly inviting him to assault that barrier. She is sensual and sexual: Olenin is always aware of her strong body "outlined against her smock" (JI 6:92); but beyond that, she is equated in his mind with nature—as an expression of the good, true, and beautiful. "Maybe in her I love nature herself," he writes, "everything beautiful that exists in nature. . . . Loving her, I feel I am an integral part of God's happy world" (JI 6:123).

The essence of Maryanka's charm and her hold on Olenin is that, although she is beautiful and flirtatious, she is, unlike the other women of the village, totally inaccessible. Even with Lukashka she is basically pristine and always virginal. When they are together, she allows him to reach into her blouse for sunflower seeds, but warns him not to "expect any nonsense" from her. When her friend Ustenka encourages her to go "into the orchards" with Lukashka, Maryanka replies: "I won't do such a stupid thing. It wouldn't be right." She is the same with Olenin. Though she leads him to believe that she is fond of him, whenever he gets close to her, she flees: "He snatched away the hand she was holding and put his arm around her young body. But she leaped up like an antelope and rushed out of the house barefoot" (JI 6:126). Olenin reveals his awe of Maryanka in a letter he writes back home: "And so every day I see before me these remote snowy mountains and this majestic happy woman" (JI 6:122). In and of nature, Maryanka and the mountains are the same: unattainable, strong, and pure. In Maryanka we clearly see the prototype of Tolstoy's later heroines, Natasha Rostov and Kitty Levin.

Olenin's love for Maryanka might appear to be a capitulation from his ascetic life to one of participation. But when Beletsky invites him to join in the party where he first really becomes acquainted with Maryanka, Olenin answers: "I would, but to tell the truth, I'm afraid of getting seriously involved" (JI 6:93). The pursuit of involvement is a problem for Olenin; he wants to be part of this world, yet something keeps him from really joining it. But by refusing to join the Cossacks in their fun Olenin can stand back and enjoy and admire the show of their freedom, particularly their sexual freedom, without testing himself. For he is plagued by a feeling that he is in any case not good enough to be really a part of the things they do. To avoid a test, he therefore had declared himself abstinent; then he had fallen in love with a girl who is, he claims, not only inaccessible to him but his superior: "I was not good enough to have straightforward, simple relations with her." Furthermore, "he seemed inexpressibly vile when he compared himself to her" (JI 6:126).

Olenin thinks of himself as "vile" and "inferior" to Maryanka because he is an erotic creature and cannot approach the unspoiled innocence which she represents. To woo Maryanka seriously and to win her would mean to succumb to the self-indulgence that Olenin wanted to escape when he came to the Caucasus. By expressing his sensuality not in his relations with her, but in his passion for hunting and for the experience of nature, Olenin keeps intact his image of Maryanka's purity while approaching the natural ideal that is its source. So that his resistance to the Cossack style of life is not so much a true asceticism as a barrier against the corruptions of his romantic vision of purity and the fusion of the erotic with the ideal.

II

"Il faut que tu crées ta femme."

Jules Michelet, *La Femme*

Although the first part of *Family Happiness* is, like *The Cossacks,* a tale of romantic love, its second half proceeds to the disillusionment with romantic love which Tolstoy foresaw but never described for Olenin and Maryanka. In this story Tolstoy conforms to his own conviction that while most love stories usually end with marriage, that is where they should begin.[4] From Masha's wedding he proceeds to her married and family life. It is the contrast between her expectations of love and the actual experience of her marriage that provides the substance and mood of the story. Beyond that, *Family Happiness* is a fictionalized treatise on the appropriate roles and behavior for women.

Eikhenbaum feels that Tolstoy was responding to contemporary feminism in *Family Happiness,* especially to three writers, Proudhon, Michelet, and Turgenev. Tolstoy certainly read Turgenev, but it is not certain that he read the attack on feminism in Proudhon's *De la Justice dans la Revolution et dans l'Église* (1858) or Jules Michelet's precious pleas for the status quo in *L'Amour* (1858) or *La Femme* (1859). (In fact, it is very unlikely that Tolstoy could have read the last before the publication of *Family Happiness* in April, 1859).

More important than the exact source of Tolstoy's inspiration is the fact that feminism was a live issue in Russian intellectual life at that time. The consequences of female anatomy, the nature of woman, the destiny of marriage, and the possibility of true equality between the sexes were all questions actively debated in publicist literature. Feminism was, moreover, not considered an isolated issue, but was connected to broad questions of social reform. Men, perhaps

4. B. M. Ejxenbaum, *Skvoz' literaturu* (Leningrad: Academia, 1924), pp. 68–69.

even more than women, wrote and talked about the new woman (as well as the new man), and their ideas on the relations of the sexes were epitomized in N. G. Chernyshevsky's *What Is To Be Done?* To what extent Tolstoy was directly involved in these debates in 1859 is unknown, but he was surely aware of them. At a dinner in St. Petersburg, he announced that George Sand should be tied to a wagon and drawn through the streets. In 1862, after the publication of *Family Happiness* and a year before the publication of *What Is To Be Done?*, Tolstoy wrote an explicitly antifeminist farce for the pleasure of his own family.[5] Of course, not only did Tolstoy bitterly resent feminist ideas, he was uncharacteristically superficial in even considering them. So much so, that Eikhenbaum's claim for *Family Happiness* as an antifeminist tract is too strong. Its main impetus came not from current public debates but from the personal dreams of domestic happiness which haunted Tolstoy at the time.

It is often asserted that *Family Happiness* is based on Tolstoy's brief flirtation with Valerya Arsenev, a young woman who lived on a neighboring estate. Even a superficial glance at their "courtship" finds a barely credible experience. Tolstoy's treatment of Valerya Arsenev was so abusive that critics often speak of *Family Happiness* as "compensatory," an apology for his constant attacks upon her appearance, her pursuits, her mind; for his fits of "love" alternating unpredictably with total rejection; and for his tantalizing talk of marriage which led to nothing.

There is no excuse for such treatment, but there is a possible explanation for it. Valerya simply did not exist as a real, live human being for Tolstoy. Potentially the manifestation of the ideal Wife and Mother, she fell far short of Tolstoy's imagined model. Painfully aware of her shortcomings, Tolstoy was able to rid himself of her as he would brush off a fly, for his intense dreams of marital happiness at the time were sufficient for him. *Family Happiness* was

5. "Zaražënnoe semejstvo," JI 7.

not based on an episode from real life. On the contrary, Tolstoy's "relationship" with Valerya was the acting out of his vision both of romantic love and its inevitable failure. In this case, Tolstoy's art did not reflect reality. Rather, his real life reflected the novella that had already taken shape in his imagination.

Before he even started *Family Happiness,* Tolstoy wrote in his diary of 1851: "At first the impulses of the heart are pure and elevated. It is reality that destroys their innocence and charm" (JI 46: 79). Nikolay Irtenev, the autobiographical hero of *Youth,* says of romantic love: "I am not speaking of the love of a young man for a young woman and vice versa. I am afraid of such endearments. I have been unfortunate enough in life not to have seen a trace of truth in that kind of love, only deception, in which sensuality, marital relations, money, a wish to bind or to free oneself have so confused any feeling itself that it has been impossible to make sense of it" (JI 2: 147). *Youth* was published two years before *Family Happiness,* in 1857, when Tolstoy was twenty-nine. His ideas about love, although they acquired different shades and tones throughout his life, did not significantly alter; indeed, they finally crystallized into a parody of Nikolay's words. In 1898 the aging author wrote to his daughter that if he could live life over again he would not get married for anything in the world:

> As for falling in love, knowing that it is not a beautiful, poetic, and lofty feeling, but a very bad and morbid one, I would not open the doors to it, but protect myself from it as carefully as we protect ourselves from far less dangerous diseases, such as diphtheria, scarlet fever, typhus. Men addicted to drugs have the same feeling, and yet they find real life only when they conquer their addictions.[6]

A year later Tolstoy provided in his diary a comment on marriage which could well serve as a gloss on *Family Happiness* and which deserves to be quoted in full:

6. Letter to T. Tolstoy quoted in Cynthia Asquith, *Married to Tolstoy* (London: Hutchinson, 1960), p. 189.

The principal cause of family unhappiness is that people are brought
up to think that marriage brings happiness. Sexual attraction leads
to marriage and it takes the form of a promise, a hope, for happiness, which is supported by public opinion and literature. But marriage is not only not happiness. It is constant suffering, which is the
price for sexual satisfaction; suffering in the form of lack of freedom, slavery, overindulgence, disgust with all kinds of spiritual and
physical defects of the mate which one has to bear—maliciousness,
stupidity, deception, vanity, drunkenness, laziness, miserliness, self-
interest and corruption—all defects which are especially difficult to
bear when they're not your own but somebody else's. And the same
with physical defects—ugliness, uncleanliness, stench, sores, insanity,
etc.—which are even more difficult to bear when not your own. All
this, or at least something of this, will always be and to bear it will
be difficult for everyone. But that which should compensate for it—
concern, satisfaction, aid—all these things are taken as a matter of
course . . . and one suffers the more from them the more one ex-
pects happiness. The principle cause of this suffering is that one ex-
pects what does not happen, and does not expect what always hap-
pens. [JI 53: 229]

Although the hysterical tone of this passage is more characteristic
of later works like *The Kreutzer Sonata,* its relation to the themes
of *Family Happiness* is clear. This lengthy observation and Tolstoy's
novella both share the conflict of romantic illusion with real experience. If the lover could hold his love to himself, his feelings would
not be endangered—"impulses of the heart are at first pure and
elevated." When the feelings are expressed, however, when they
explicitly seek and join their natural object, then "reality destroys
their innocence and charm." Reality, in this view, is not only moral
and physical defects, the stench and sores and disillusion of living
together with the loved one. Reality is also the mandate to surrender
a fantasy born in one's imagination over which one has perfect
control, a dream of perfection of the self and of the mate and of a
shared life. Although Masha finds partial relief in her eventual re-

turn to the preoccupations and discipline of family life, both she and Sergey are portrayed as victims of a doomed illusion.

The first sentence of Masha's story—"I was then seventeen"— invokes the tension between her youth and her maturity, and invites the reader's indulgence for what is to follow. The atmosphere of her seventeenth year is filled with the cold of winter and grief over her mother's death. Sheltered from the greater world by her rural life and her womanhood, Masha is dejected, lonely, and bored; like Olenin, she finds no meaning in her life and this frustration leads her to continual tears and abraded nerves. Masha is, moreover, ripe for the crowning experience of especially female adolescence—romantic love. Her reacquaintance, therefore, with Sergey Mikhailych, an old friend of the family, inspires in Masha incipient love and all the dreams that go with it. Yet from her later perspective this process is extremely difficult for her to remember, and when remembered, impossible to describe: "I find it difficult now to recall and understand the dreams which then filled my imagination. Even when I can recall them, I find it hard to believe that my dreams were like that: they were so strange and so removed from life" (JI 5: 73).

After she meets Sergey Mikhailych, Masha's behavior is a caricature of the young girl in love:

> I often went into the garden and wandered for a long time alone through the paths, or sat on a bench there; and heaven knows what my thoughts and wishes and hopes were at such times. Sometimes at night, especially if there was a moon, I sat by my bedroom window till dawn; sometimes . . . I stole out into the garden wearing only a robe and ran through the dew as far as the pond; and once I went all the way to the open fields and walked all around the garden alone at night. [JI 5: 73]

In reading this account, one feels that Tolstoy's heroine is not describing her memory of events so much as she is describing Tolstoy's fantasy of how a young girl in love behaves. Her actions are, in short, archetypal rather than individual. And the reader is led to share the incredulity and incomprehension which the mature Masha (as she narrates the story) feels toward the "remembered" actions of the young Masha, falling in love.

When they first meet, Sergey Mikhailych himself provides the foil to Masha's intoxication with the idea of love. Older, more experienced, he answers her fantasies with a sober-minded realism. At first, Sergey Mikhailych tries to maintain a paternal relation to Masha. He is, after all, an old friend of her father's and his attempts to substitute for him are both natural and successful. When he discovers that Masha is suffering from melancholy, Sergey rightly sees it as "the most important thing of all," diagnosing it as incapacity for solitude and a lack of inner resources (JI 5:71). As therapy, he prescribes music, books, study, and he orders her to fill her time constructively while he is away on business. Fulfilling his promise later to "examine" her on the uses made of her time, he inquires and discovers that she has not been idle, bored, or depressed during his absence (JI 5:72). Formally, he plays her father, giving praise "as to a child." Correspondingly, animated by an instinct for full honesty with him, Masha feels compelled to tell him not only her "good" actions but also—"as if I were in church"—her "bad" ones (JI 5:74).

Yet Sergey Mikhailych is only half right in his diagnosis of Masha's adolescent melancholy; it is not only her time that is empty, but her heart, too. In the excitement and incipient love of her initial encounter with Sergey Mikhailych, Masha feels not merely that her "dejection would pass off, but that it had already passed off, or rather, had never existed." Upon discovering him, Masha lost the feeling of meaninglessness—"I had ceased to ask that terrible question, what is the good of it all?"—and became convinced of the basic principle that "the proper object of life was happiness." And with this discovery, Masha's house became "full of light and life" (JI 5: 72–73).

It soon becomes evident, then, that Sergey Mikhailych will aban-

don his fiction as second parent and surrender to his growing feeling for Masha. Yet Sergey Mikhailych regards his own preference
for "sitting still" as one of his disqualifications for marriage. Despite the frequency of marriages between mature men and very
young girls in nineteenth-century Russia, Sergey Mikhailych sounds
convincing when he asserts that his marrying moment has passed;
for the sober maturity of thirty-six does not seem to him reconcilable
with a seventeen-year-old's thirst and need for experience. In a conversation with the family about marriage, he announces that it
would be a misfortune for a girl of seventeen to marry a man of his
age. He contrasts the "old worn out man who only wants to stand
still" with the heart of a girl in which "heaven knows what wishes
are fermenting." He goes so far as to say explicitly that a marriage
between himself and Masha "would be a misfortune" (JI 5: 75). To
this statement Masha replies with a denial—and one may conclude
that Sergey Mikhailych has stated his position not only to express a
real conviction but also to be contradicted and ultimately defeated
in argument with the seventeen-year-old girl. One is scarcely surprised when Masha's initial objections to his view are overridden by
Sergey's own fearful avoidance of the full confrontation with her
and by his eagerness to force her admission that such a marriage
could not be good. He then closes the issue firmly by adding that
for himself also "it would be a very great misfortune" (JI 5: 76).

The actual proposal that Sergey Mikhailych does make is extraordinarily convoluted. Its indirectness accords with the hesitancy
and lack of initiative that characterized his courtship. Sergey Mikhailych begins by explaining to Masha that a fictitious character "A"
(he himself) must leave a fictitious character "B" (Masha) because
he no longer loves her as a daughter, but as a woman. That young
woman, moreover, thinks of life as a toy—she is young and naive,
he is old and hardened, and he, in a word, is afraid of her. A poi-
gnantly accurate picture of their future emerges from Sergey's further
remarks: "The other story is that she took pity on him, imagined,

poor child, from her ignorance of the world, that she really could love him, and so consented to be his wife. And he, in his madness, believed it—believed that his whole life could begin again; but she saw herself that she had deceived him and that he had deceived her. . . . But let us drop the subject" (JI 5:96). The intensity and the aggressiveness of Masha's reply to Sergey surprise even Masha herself. She suggests that "There is a third ending to the story; the third ending is that he did not love her, but hurt her, hurt her, and thought that he was right; and he left her and was actually proud of himself. You have been pretending, not I; I have loved you since the first day we met, loved you" (JI 5:97). Masha's challenge to Sergey in this scene substitutes for his doubt and hesitancy an assurance and initiative of her own. This basic urge toward independence and her own identity will threaten the harmony of Masha's marriage and is clearly suggested even before Sergey's proposal.

During their courtship, Sergey and Masha, with her sister Sonya, go off one day to pick cherries. They find the orchard locked. While Sonya disappears to fetch the key, Sergey climbs the wall and enters the orchard. In pursuit of the luscious fruit, he has penetrated a sanctum, the locked garden of delights. Yet there is more in Tolstoy's evocation than the penetration of a forbidden garden, and more than a psychoanalytic significance. For Masha, the locked orchard suddenly becomes Eve's proving ground.

From inside the wall, Sergey Mikhailych calls out, "If you want some, give me the dish." Masha replies, "No, I want to pick for myself" (JI 5:83–84). Overcome by curiosity to see him inside his sanctuary, Masha scales the wall and sees Sergey within, transfigured into a pure lover of radiant intensity. The burden of his years and his skepticism have dropped away in the privacy and beauty of the orchard. When he realizes that Masha is watching him, he has become a young man, innocent of the knowledge which had made him believe a marriage with her unsuitable or impossible. But precisely then, at the sight of her lover's perfect tranquility, Masha explains that "the same instant brought an irresistible desire to upset his composure again and test my power over him" (JI 5: 84–85). And with that, though he forbids it, Masha leaps down into the garden and begins to pick cherries.

This encounter ends in silence and embarrassment. Masha, hurt by the return of "the old uncle who spoiled or scolded," feels compelled to defy and hurt him. Sergey, in his turn confused and upset, fails to seize this moment for the articulation and resolution of their mutual feelings. "He tried to drop into his fatherly, patronizing manner again," Masha says, "but he did not fool me" (JI 5: 85). His double failure—to break down barriers, and to cope with her wish for direct experience of life—will continue in their marriage. And Masha will continue to disturb his "paradise." Much later Sergey Mikhailych reproaches his wife for "sharing the dirtiness and idleness and luxury of this foolish society." But Masha, contrary to her expressed wish to hear the truth from her husband, interprets his brutally honest words as an effort to dominate her. Echoing her defiance of Sergey in the cherry orchard, she promises herself that, though "such may be a husband's rights," she "will not submit to them."

If Sergey's proposal lacked force, the wedding ceremony which followed is even less promising. The differences between the wedding of Masha and Sergey and that of Levin and Kitty in *Anna Karenina,* the only other described in detail, are striking. First, one crude distinction: Tolstoy thinks Levin's marriage is good, and Masha's bad; more precisely, he believes Masha's marriage flawed by grievously delusive expectations. The way each begins is very different and forecasts the nature of the marriages themselves.

Kitty and Levin are married in an elegant Moscow church, crowded with friends and relatives. Though it is true that Tolstoy did not like cities, Moscow, mother city of Russia and of decent tradition, was least disagreeable to him. Moreover, Moscow symbol-ized national stability and security to Tolstoy and, indeed, to any Russian. And, as the site of their marriage, Moscow graciously lends something of those qualities to Kitty and Levin's marriage. During their wedding ceremony, a feeling of joy pervades everything they do. "Kitty gazed at everybody with the same unseeing eyes as Levin. To everything that was said to her she could only reply with a smile of happiness which was so natural to her now" (JI 19:17). Further on, Levin wonders if Kitty shares his understanding of the words of the ceremony but "she could not listen to them or understand them, so powerful was the one feeling which filled her soul and which was growing stronger and stronger. It was a feeling of joy at the full fruition of what had been going on in her soul for the last month and a half and what had during those six weeks gladdened and worried her" (JI 19:17). Another passage repeats this triumphant picture of Kitty: "Kitty listened to the words of the prayer, trying to understand their meaning but unable to do so. A feeling of triumph and radiant joy filled her heart more and more as the ceremony proceeded and robbed her of her ability to attend to it." As for Levin, he feels as "bright and happy as she did" (JI 19:24).

Even more important in Levin's case is that he is struck with awe at the new responsibility he is assuming: "All the bother about his shirt, about being late, his conversations with friends and relations, their displeasure, his ridiculous position—all suddenly vanished and he felt happy and terrified." Further on, Levin thinks: "What do I know? What can I do in this awful matter without help? Yes, it is indeed help that I want now" (JI 19:18–19).

As Kitty and Levin proceed through the ritual, they "enjoyed hearing the reading of the epistle. . . . They enjoyed drinking the warm red wine and water from the shallow cup, and they liked it even more when the priest, throwing back his chasuble and taking their hands in his, led them around the lectern while a bass voice chanted *Rejoice, O Isaiah*" (JI 19:25). And they, in this way, endow the ceremony with meaning: that is, the value of it, as a Tolstoyan sacrament, proceeds from them to it, not vice versa. In this sometimes humorous depiction of their wedding, Tolstoy portrays with great warmth Kitty's and Levin's joy and fear in the face of this terrible and mysterious new responsibility. This treatment, elevated, and full of promise, embodies Tolstoy's hopes for their marriage. For Kitty and Levin have not merely shared a sacrament, they have both experienced a conversion.

In contrast, Masha's wedding proves to be the first sign of the "end of her romance." The site of her wedding is a quiet, almost empty, country chapel, which only a few hours before had been the scene of a memorial service for Masha's father. It is not propitious that a death has been commemorated on their wedding day. And while Kitty and Levin are fully aware of each other, for Masha her groom barely exists; she "feels his presence" beside her, but does not look at him. Masha's reactions to the ceremony are all, without exception, bleak and grimly disappointed, uncomprehending and cold. She finds that "nothing in her soul responded to the words of the prayers"; she is "unable to pray"; she looks "listlessly" at the icons; and she feels that "something strange" is being done to her. The priest and guests congratulate the newlyweds, but Masha is only "frightened and disappointed"; even worse, she feels that "nothing extraordinary, nothing worthy of the sacrament [she] had just received, had happened within [her]." When she and her husband kiss, their kiss seems "strange, and not expressive of [their] feeling." The mutual joy, the solemn vision and the transformation that informs Kitty and Levin's wedding is absent from Masha's. Her disappointment leads Masha to ask , "Is this all there is to this moment from which I expected so much?" (JI 5: 104). Her wedding, ironically, initiates the gradual disillusion that finally destroys the romantic core of her marriage.

At first, the future that Sergey and Masha had imagined seems both charming and attainable. Sergey had assured Masha that "now I think I have found what is needed for happiness. A quiet secluded life in the country, with the possibility of being useful to people to whom it is easy to do good, and who are not accustomed to it; then work, which one hopes may be of some use; then rest, nature, books, music, love for one's neighbor—such is my idea of happiness. And then, on top of all that, you for a mate, and children, perhaps—that is all a man can wish for."

"It should be enough," [Masha] replied. [JI 5: 100]

Much earlier Masha had confessed that

now I understood why [Sergey] said that happiness is only living for another, and I agree with him completely. It seemed to me that we would be peacefully and endlessly happy together. And I didn't imagine trips abroad, or a glittering social life, but a completely different, quiet family life in the country with constant self-sacrifice, with enduring love for one another, and with the continuing awareness of a beneficent providence. [JI 5: 93]

This idyll reflects the perfect concordance of spirit and purpose that Tolstoy envisioned in his own future marriage.

As first, Masha's marriage is, indeed, far more happy than she and Sergey had dreamed. The newlyweds dote on each other, play like children, and love like foolish sweethearts. The nature of their life, however, is different from what they had imagined: "Our dreams about how we would manage our country life turned out to be completely different than we expected. But our life was no worse than our plans" (JI 5: 105). Their plans for "hard work, performance of duty, self-sacrifice, and life for others" are replaced by "a selfish feeling of love for one another, a wish to be loved, a constant irrational gaiety and oblivion to the whole world" (JI 5: 105). Though they are happy together, their early love does not widen their responsibilities but turns inward to the enchanting but selfish pursuit of pleasure.

This failure of expectation is soon followed by an increasing restlessness and dissatisfaction in Masha which quickly develops into depression and fits of resentment directed toward her husband. She experiences what Tolstoy later in life described in a note to his son's fiancée: "To you, Sonya, I say this: you will suddenly find yourself bored, oh, so bored, so bored, so bored. Do you believe in it, do not submit to it; be assured that it is not boredom but your spirit's simple demand for work, any kind, physical, intellectual, it's all the same" (JI 64: 160). But Sergey Mikhailych refuses to admit Masha to the "mysterious realm" of the problems and concerns which were a central part of his masculine world. Although Masha at first accepted this, and regarded it as natural, she finally rebels against the silence between them in the crucial area of the convictions, plans, and hopes that occupy her husband's time. And Sergey Mikhailych's failure to try once again to rehabilitate Masha may well predict Tolstoy's later view that "there exists the current naive belief that a husband, especially if he is older than his wife, and his wife is very young, can develop and educate her. That is a gross error. . . . Women live completely independently of a man's spiritual life . . . and never submit to the influence of their husbands; but they themselves, by way of their stubbornness and cunning, indirectly influence everything . . . including men" (JI 54: 22).

Though they dreamed of an idyllic life in the country, Sergey had expressed his doubt to Masha that that would be enough for her— "You have youth and beauty," he says. To Tolstoy, the frivolity and vanity that accompany youth and beauty, especially in women, are in conflict with peace and stability. They have an existential logic of their own which is essentially uncongenial to domestic happiness. And Sergey Mikhailych's doubts about the difference in their expectations gradually materialize: his, the hope of an older man for a peacefully productive life in the country and hers, the potential wish of a young girl for a glamorous social life. Left alone with her thoughts, Masha suddenly becomes aware that "to love him was not enough for me after the happiness I had felt in falling in love."

From this first disenchantment, she moves to a more urgent craving for tension and excitement: "I wanted movement and not a calm course of existence. I wanted excitement and danger and the chance to sacrifice myself for my love" (JI 5: 110). Her youth and beauty begin, as her husband had feared, to demand their rights. She complains that she "doesn't want to play at life, but to live" like her husband himself (JI 5: 113).

Sergey surrenders to this demand and suggests a trip to St. Petersburg. There, Masha falls eager victim to the craving of an idle cosmopolitan society for novelty and excitement, and, thanks to her "rural simplicity and charm," becomes an instant social success. Initially, Sergey Mikhailych is proud of her social grace and winning ways: "Everybody is delighted with her," he writes his mother. "I can't admire her enough myself and should be more in love with her than ever, if that were possible" (JI 5: 117). This initial delight thins, however, as Masha becomes more and more involved in high society and their return to the quiet life of Nikolskoe seems less and less a possibility. Masha mistakes her social success for an estimation of her human worth, and comes to think of high society as a career and life in itself. More and more it seems to her that she is the "center around which everything revolved" (JI 5: 118).

As the gulf between them widens, Sergey and Masha openly express their mutual dissatisfaction. Outraged at her disengagement from him, Sergey accuses Masha of "forgetting her womanly dignity" (JI 5: 122). Finally, dangerously out of touch, poisoned with concealed resentments and bitter silences, Masha confesses that they "had long ceased to be the most perfect people in the world to one another, but made comparisons with others and secretly judged one another" (JI 5: 125).

Events that are supposed to draw husbands and wives closer together fail to narrow the gulf that separates Sergey and Masha. The birth of their first child encourages no rapprochement; Sergey Mikhailych alone is affected by the birth of this baby and, by taking

a motherly role in his son's life, fills the vacuum that Masha has left.
Masha, for whom caring for her child becomes "mere habit and
the routine performance of duty," often finds her husband in the
nursery with the child as she comes in to say goodnight before going off to a ball (JI 5: 127). Though he says nothing, she seems to
see her own self-reproach reflected in his eyes.

By this time, Masha has frankly admitted that "fashionable life
which had dazzled me at first by its glitter and its flattery of my
vanity, soon captured all of my inclinations and occupied all of my
soul, so that there was no room left for feeling" (JI 5: 126). Virtu-
ally living an independent life of her own, Masha makes a trip to
Baden, which provides a turning point in her life. At the beginning
of her stay at the resort, she is in excellent spirits; she is young,
lovely, chic, and constantly surrounded by men. She does not love
any of them, nor distinguish one from the other, but she is by now
addicted to their flattery.

Masha's brilliant career, however, is destined to end at Baden. For
her admirers find a new pet in an equally brilliant and beautiful
Englishwoman. Forgotten, disillusioned, and bored once again,
Masha seeks the companionship of a Russian woman with whom she
finds real friendship. They one day ride into the country and talk
frankly about the emptiness of the life at Baden, their family life,
and their native land. Wandering through an abandoned castle they
meet an Italian marquis who has distinguished himself by his per-
sistence and daring in pursuing Masha. In a secluded part of the
castle the marquis tries to embrace and kiss Masha.

Many things, according to her own narrative, go through her
mind at that moment, including horror and disgust with the marquis and herself, along with an equally strong desire to "surrender
[herself] to the kisses of that coarse handsome mouth, and to the
embrace of those white hands with their delicate veins and jewelled
fingers." In her own heart, she cries, "Go ahead! Let me be covered
with even more sin and shame!" (JI 5: 132). For the moment Masha

wants to surrender to her imagined lover of the romantic dream she had earlier described: "If only I could go with him to the edge of the abyss and say, 'one step, and I shall fall over—one moment, and I shall be lost!' then, pale with fear, he would catch me in his strong arms and hold me over the edge till my blood froze, and then carry me off wherever he pleased" (JI 5: 111). But that former dream suddenly seems as empty as the abandoned castle in which her romance is staged. Masha's thoughts suddenly turn to her family and she flees to her husband in Heidelberg.

The story does not end there, however; for although Sergey and Masha return to the country, the distance between them seems even greater in the setting of their early dream of marital happiness. Masha observes that "they sensed in their relations the familiar discipline of manners. We lived our separate lives; he had his own occupations in which I was not needed and which I no longer wished to share, while I continued my idle life which no longer vexed or grieved him. The children were still too young to form a bond between us" (JI 5: 134).

But that first summer back at Nikolskoe does bring a resolution to Sergey and Masha's emotional stalemate. Encouraged by the gentle promise of a summer shower and a moment of tenderness, Masha asks her husband if he does not regret the past. Reluctantly, Sergey answers that he does regret the loss of their former love, but that he had been successful in destroying "that which tormented me." When Masha asks why Sergey did not exercise his authority and "lock her up," he replies that "all of us, and especially you women, must have personal experience of all the nonsense of life in order to get back to life itself; it is impossible to learn from someone else. At that time you had not yet exhausted that charming nonsense, which I admired in you, though my own time for that sort of thing was long past" (JI 5: 141). The reply is unsatisfying, for it implies that the experience necessary to wisdom inevitably destroys the purpose of wisdom: to understand, to love, and to live richly. And it is particularly obtuse about the impossibility of direct experience, without penalty, for women.

Sergey ends their conversation by exhorting Masha to be thankful for what they have had, and to "stand aside and make room" for the new generation, represented by their children. When he kisses her in conclusion of their talk, Masha sees "not a lover any longer but an old friend" (JI 5: 142). This is a reversion to their earliest relations and draws the full circle of their romance. They have grown into the roles of their parents before them, into a style of life that was imprinted upon them in early youth.

Though it is far different from the happiness they had dreamed of, Sergey and Masha do achieve a kind of family happiness, if not a rich relationship with one another. In the final paragraph, Masha remarks that the long-delayed frank conversation with her husband ended the "romance" of their marriage, and that an eternal triangle —mother, father, children—took its place: "A new feeling of love for my children and the father of my children laid the foundation of a new but completely different happiness in life which has lasted until now" (JI 5: 143). This "quite different happiness" is a result of the late conversion from self-interest to the extended concerns of marriage and family, and especially from *eros* to *agape*.

The message concerning their mutual failures and responsibilities is clear. In an ideal marriage, the wife is in fact "created" by her husband, responds to his teaching, and identifies solely with his interests and well-being. He, in turn, provides a safe and secure setting for her continued dependence and must counter with stern discipline her need to control her own life. Yet Tolstoy recognizes the futility of achieving this "ideal" and, in contrast to later works on the same themes, is remarkably sensitive to the failures and virtues of both his hero and heroine. Masha develops as a naive, vain, and misguided young woman, but she is only potentially an archetypal destructress like Ellen Kuragin. Yet Masha is clearly the partner who most seriously endangers the marriage. Sergey Mikhailych is portrayed consistently as sober, rational, and mature—guilty only of too much compassion.

By virtue of its style and technique, *Family Happiness* is a tour de force. The story itself is rudimentary and serves more as a backdrop to interior drama than as a stage-setting for dramatic action. By the absence of significant dramatic incident, Tolstoy emphasizes the importance which he attaches to the development of his heroine's consciousness. In this respect, the proper ancestor of *Family Happiness* is the high subjectivity of Stendhal, and its heir is the psychological novel of the twentieth century. It shares this characteristic with some portions of Dostoevsky's *Notes from the Underground,* and those other works of Dostoevsky—*Poor Folk,* for example—in which the real drama lies within the narrator's consciousness.

It is extraordinary that the man who was to become the patriarch of Russian literature, representing in his life and in his literary image an acrid masculinity, tells his story through the consciousness of a delicately bred girl. This memoir of her youth refracts through the prism of feminine perceptions the world of Masha's most rapid emotional development. Thanks to the first-person point of view, we know far more about the minute processes of Masha's psyche and developing awareness than we do about Natasha Rostov's or Ellen Kuragin's or Anna Karenina's. This concentrated and sustained representation of the psychological and emotional reality of a woman's consciousness is in all of Tolstoy a unique attempt.

Eikhenbaum argues that *Family Happiness* is, finally, an unsuccessful novel.[7] He cites among other defects its inconsistencies of style, its schematic nature, its concealed polemical motives. One year before writing *Family Happiness* Tolstoy had written in his diary, "[Turgenev's] *Asya* is garbage."[8] Masha, Eikhenbaum suggests, is partially an antitype to Turgenev's semi-emancipated heroines. But while Tolstoy was deeply hostile to the Turgenev heroine, accord-

7. See Ejxenbaum's general discussion above, note 1.
8. Ejxenbaum, *Lev Tolstoj,* vol. 1, p. 345.

ing to Eikhenbaum he wanted to show in *Family Happiness* that
he could rival Turgenev's delicate poetic prose style, so alien to
his own.

These observations may be valid, but they do not constitute an
artistic failure. The schematic quality of Masha's memoir is at
least partially due to a literary or contrived notion of experience
that in Tolstoy is the substance of romantic love. It is what is meant
when Princess Betsy says to Anna Karenina that Anna is a "real
heroine out of a novel." The lush passages in *Family Happiness*
which refer in detail to all the little petals of a flower and the exact
tone of a nightingale's song heighten this artificial sensibility and
serve not to rival Turgenev but to parody him and his heroines.

The real Tolstoy and his real themes are, however, apparent in
other kinds of nature studies in *Family Happiness*. For example,
Tolstoy paints the "natural" background to Masha's wedding day
with great care, concentrating on its coldness, meagerness, and
decline. The day before the wedding was "our first autumn evening, bright and cold. Everything was wet, cold, and shining, and
the garden showed for the first time the spaciousness and color and
bareness of autumn. The sky was clear, cold, and pale" (JI 5: 101).
Masha wakes on her wedding day, walks out into the garden, and
sees the "almost leafless, yellowing lime trees along the walk." The
frostbitten leaves of the mountain ash are crumpled and the berries
hang "wrinkled" on the boughs. The dahlias are black and
wrinkled; around the house the burdock plants are broken (JI 5:
101).

On their way to attend a memorial service for Masha's father,
she and Sergey Mikhailych note the "bare fields and pale sky, from
which the bright but powerless rays, trying to burn [her] cheek,
fell over all the landscape" (JI 5: 102). The footpath is covered
with "beaten and trampled stubble"; the stubble extends to a "leafless wood." The world is silent too: "our voices and footsteps were
the only sounds," and in the distance a peasant was "noiselessly

ploughing a black strip which grew wider and wider. . . . The winter sun shone over everything," and "when we spoke, the sound of our voices hung in the motionless air above us, as if we two were alone in the whole world—alone under that blue arch, lighted by the flashing and glimmering of the heatless sun" (JI 5: 103).

There is none of Turgenev's lyricism in these passages. The cold, meager, exhausted landscape of autumn is suggestive of the wasteland of Masha's marriage. There is no heat in the winter sun just as there will be no romantic passion left in Masha's love for Sergey or his for her. The concrete, evocative style in these passages is characteristic of Tolstoy's best writing.

Yet *Family Happiness* has been unfairly neglected, and remains unappreciated as the important and moving work that it is. This is undoubtedly related to the fact that it represents an atypical attempt in nineteenth-century Russian literature by a male writer to write from a female point of view, exclusively through a feminine consciousness. It is a successful attempt insofar as women perceive it to be "true." [9] Male critics, however, have been less responsive to this female perspective and, perhaps because is was so extraordinary an attempt, have never discussed the question of female point of view directly.

V. P. Botkin, a critic and friend, wrote to Tolstoy that the "failure" of *Family Happiness* resulted from a "vagueness" in its basic theme. He complains that "the point of the novella remained obscure." [10] And Eikhenbaum attributes its structure, "the notes of a woman on her life," to the author's "substitution of style (poetic) for concrete material." [11] The masculine prejudice that equates the lyrical with femininity and the realistic with masculinity is surely operative in these two judgments. More important, however, is the failure to

9. Women students in courses I have taught have remarked on Tolstoy's uncanny ability to write "like a woman."
10. Ejxenbaum, *Lev Tolstoj,* vol. 1, p. 360.
11. *Ibid.,* p. 361.

see *Family Happiness* as Tolstoy's only attempt to write from the inner world of consciousness outward. As such, its private and personal perspective is perfectly appropriate to the memoirs of a young woman, since the external world, and the growth that comes from living in it, are closed to her. Although Tolstoy is by no means sympathetic to Masha's brief emergence into that world, he captures the moods that shape her frustrated life. Because this was so rare for the period (and is even now), men were and are not likely to perceive its "point" as significant, or regard female experience as the legitimate substance of moving literature.

One sees clearly in this novella some major themes of the great novels: the disappointing contrast between the ideal and the real; the destructive and limiting power of romantic love; the breakdown of communication between man and wife; and the hope for building a common bond in the purgation of sex and the redeeming discipline of family life. It is significant that, at the age of thirty-one when he still entertained the possibility of a happy marriage and family life, Tolstoy could write with such perception about the failure of this vision. (Other later marriages, Natasha's, and Levin's, for example, turn out much better.) But *Family Happiness* clearly marks the first step on the way toward Anna and Karenin, and toward the final despair of Pozdnyshev in *The Kreutzer Sonata* which causes him to confess that "in the depths of my soul I felt from the first weeks that I was lost, that things had not turned out as I expected, that not only was marriage no happiness, but a very heavy burden; but like everybody else, I did not wish to acknowledge this to myself. . ." (Jl 27: 33).

In *Family Happiness,* Tolstoy is concerned not only with the private aspects of marriage and family life, but with the society in which marriage must survive. In contrast to the mythical quality of the exotic society of *The Cossacks,* here Tolstoy portrays with palpable force the more familiar and, in his hands, more substantial Russian country and city life of the mid-nineteenth century. Bitterly portrayed in *Anna Karenina,* that society, distracting by virtue of its quest for novelty, and corrupting by virtue of its appetite for sensuality, poses a constant threat to the harmony and stability of marriage. But because Tolstoy in 1859 had not as yet achieved the breadth and depth of the masterpieces, *Family Happiness* describes more the private and personal failure of a vision of happiness than the social ambiance that contributed to it.

Before Tolstoy proceeded from Masha to Anna, however, the figure of Natasha Rostov intervened. If Masha can be considered an antitype to Turgenev's heroines, Natasha is a response to the urge toward independence and self-realization that characterized Masha and flawed her marriage. Although even Natasha does not escape Tolstoy's ambivalence toward women, she is his most popular heroine and the one he believed to be most suited to create a true family happiness.

THREE

Two Natashas

> [Natasha] writes little poems in her album, understands
> and values friendship and family life.
> She's charming, enchanting, but she doesn't have depth.
> . . . She has two great failings: vanity and a passion for
> flattery; and an aimless coquetry that has no limits.
>
> From the drafts of *War and Peace*

In his characterization of Natasha Rostov, Tolstoy states some of
the most important themes of *War and Peace.* In her, life fights
against death, humanity against materialism, spontaneity against
manipulation, intuition against reason, endurance and continuity
against disorder and chaos, private experience against civic, and
truth against disguise. In short, Tolstoy has created a conventionally
positive and sympathetic heroine. But because Tolstoy identifies
Natasha's most attractive qualities and roles specifically with her
womanhood, his attitudes toward her are colored by his ambivalent
views of women in general. Not even Natasha fully escapes the
"implacable hostility" toward women that Gorky saw in Tolstoy.[1]

Crucial to Natasha's character is her nonintellectual temperament.
In one of his sketches for *War and Peace,* Tolstoy describes Natasha
as "stupid, but nice, uneducated, knows nothing . . ." (JI 13:18).
Natasha's nonintellectuality, her lack of formal education, and her
political naiveté serve a polemical purpose: these traits challenge the
achievements and the aspirations of the feminists of the 1860s.[2]

1. Gorkij, *Lev Tolstoj,* p. 265.
2. See chap. 1, note 39.

As suggested in the introduction, Tolstoy thought that women should not be involved with political and social problems; they had a more important function to fulfill at home in serving their husbands and educating their children. Masha of *Family Happiness,* for example, seriously endangered her marriage by living independently of her husband and children.

Aside from polemics, there are motives internal to the novel which caused Tolstoy to draw Natasha as an intuitive "feminine" figure rather than as an articulate intellectual. Tolstoy was suspicious of woman's use of words. Late in life, he wrote in his diary: "Women do not use words to express their thoughts, but to attain their goals . . ." (JI 53: 178–79). So that Natasha's inarticulate nature escapes the stigma of calculating self-interest that Tolstoy associated with a woman's facile tongue. In *War and Peace* there are countless instances of Natasha's difficulty in articulating her thoughts. The first time she appears, she talks incoherently and brokenly about her doll:

> As she laughed she uttered some incoherent phrases about the doll which was poking out from her petticoat.
> "Do you see? . . . My doll . . . Mimi . . . you see. . . . " And Natasha could say no more, it all seemed so funny to her. [JI 9: 47]

Much later in the book, before the battle of Borodino, Andrey recalls an evening with Natasha in Petersburg:

> Natasha with an eager, excited face had been telling him how in looking for mushrooms the previous summer she had lost her way in a great forest. She described incoherently the dark depths of the forest, her feelings, and her talk with a beekeeper she met, and she repeatedly interrupted her story, saying: "No, I can't, I'm not describing it properly; no you won't understand me. . . ." Natasha was not satisfied with her own words; she felt that they did not convey the passionately poetical feeling she had known that day and tried to express. [JI 11: 212]

This passage adds an important dimension to this aspect of Natasha's nature. She feels that words, which should ideally be ordered and precise, cannot possibly render what she experiences intuitively. To Natasha, of all the women in *War and Peace,* belongs a straight, true intuition of things. After Anna Mikhailovna and her father have learned about Nikolay's wound, Natasha senses that they have some kind of secret—because, as Tolstoy writes, she was "of all the family the one most gifted with the talent for catching the nuances of intonation, glances, and expressions . . ." (JI 9: 282). This passage is reminiscent of Tolstoy's description in *Youth* of the special kind of understanding (*ponimanie*) which existed between Nikolay Irtenev and his brother. *Ponimanie,* as defined there, depends least of all on verbalization, and most of all on intuitive response to tone of voice, expression, and gesture.

As if to compensate for her inarticulateness, Tolstoy endows Natasha with a penetrating vision which strips other characters of pose and pretense. Once again Natasha's first appearance reveals this basic gift. Young Natasha, provoked by the condescending tone of a simpering guest, "did not respond, but stared solemnly at her" (JI 9: 282). Again, four years later, when Boris reestablishes relations with the Rostovs in Petersburg, Natasha scrutinizes him carefully as he talks to her mother:

> He felt oppressed by that persistent, friendly gaze and glanced once or twice at her. . . . The uniform, the spurs, the tie, the way Boris had brushed his hair—it was all fashionable and *comme il faut.* That Natasha noticed at once.

And further along in the same scene:

> Natasha sat silently the whole time, looking up from under her brows at him. Her eyes made Boris more and more uneasy and embarrassed. . . . Still, the same curious, provocative and rather mocking eyes gazed at him. [JI 10: 189]

Fresh from Moscow, she sees through the glittering pretensions Boris has acquired in Petersburg.

This special faculty of Natasha's suggests that she has a direct, intuitive link with certain basic truths not accessible to ordinary people, a faculty typically associated with "earth-women" in literature. Tolstoy turns this gift to deeper thematic purpose in the famous scene following the chase at the home of the Rostovs' uncle.

When Natasha arrived with Nikolay at Mikhailovka, the peasants there called her "A regular Tatar woman!" (JI 10:261). This epithet echoes the nickname "Cossack," which Marya Dmitriyevna assigned to Natasha early in the book (JI 9:73), and it clearly associates her with a primitive, earthy world. Indeed, the mysterious peasant woman, Anisya Fyodorovna; the crude but ample fare of biscuits, honey, nuts, mushrooms; the fresh simple music of the uncle's balalaika that draws Natasha to her feet—everything about the uncle's home creates the right setting for Natasha's full emergence in her dance as a woman inherently tied to the very earth and air of Russia:

> Where, how, when had this young countess, educated by a French emigrée, absorbed with the Russian air she breathed the spirit of that dance? Where had she picked up these movements which the *pas de chale* should have long ago erased? But the spirit, the motions were those inimitable, unteachable Russian gestures the uncle had hoped for from her. . . .
>
> She danced the dance well, so well indeed, so perfectly, that Anisya Fyodorovna . . . had tears in her eyes, though she laughed as she watched that slender, graceful little countess, reared in silk and velvet, belonging to another world than hers, who was nonetheless able to understand all that was in Anisya and her father and her mother and her aunt and every native Russian. [JI 10:266]

From this scene, a comparison has been drawn between Natasha and Pushkin's Tatyana as heroines "'Russian at heart', familiar

with the customs and traditions of popular Russian life. . . ." [3] But
the point of the scene is precisely that Natasha is *not* familiar with
popular Russian life. She simply knows instinctively how to do the
dance. The appropriate literary parallel is not Pushkin's Tatyana,
but Tolstoy's own nature-girl, Maryanka of *The Cossacks*. This
passage identifies Natasha not only with the Russian "folk"—
specifically with the peasants who live close to nature—but allegori-
cally with a life unspoiled by civilization.

Natasha's innocence precludes any interest in the sophisticated
political and social issues which are constantly discussed around her
and which shape her life. At the grand ball in Petersburg, for
example, Natasha is completely oblivious to the high politics being
negotiated there: "She noticed nothing and saw nothing of what
was absorbing everyone else at the ball. She did not notice that the
Tsar talked a long time with the French ambassador. . . . She did
not even see the Tsar, and noticed that he was gone only because
the ball became livelier after his departure" (JI 10: 203).

On one level Natasha's indifference is simply a normal reaction
to the glitter of her first big ball. But beyond that, her instinct
for the private and the immediate constitutes for Tolstoy the appropriate female balance to the pompous games of male diplomats. In
a later and more intense scene of national disaster, her utter un-
concern as the Rostovs leave Moscow might be considered grossly
insensitive and inappropriate to the grave occasion: "Natasha had
rarely experienced such a joyful feeling as she had at that moment
sitting in the carriage by the countess and watching, as they slowly
moved by her, the walls of forsaken, agitated Moscow" (JI 11: 320).
But Natasha's reactions are seldom unsuitable; her joyful mood
at a time of crisis for the Russian people has another source: the
tacit assumption, the inner faith, that she and her family and other

3. R. F. Christian, *Tolstoy's "War and Peace"* (Oxford: Clarendon Press,
1962), pp. 98–99.

Russians and Russia are too strong and too good to perish, that the Rostovs' home may burn, but the Rostovs and Russia will endure. Surely this is Tolstoy's implication when, describing the imminent collapse of Moscow, he writes: "In the staid and decorous house of the Rostovs the collapse of all the usual conditions of life was very slightly perceptible" (JI 11 : 320).

Thus, when one considers Natasha's most apparent qualities, one sees a positive world: her normal response to life is: Yes. And Tolstoy constantly poses her instinct for affirmation against the values of the characters he despises. Natasha's first appearance not only underscores some of her most important qualities (her spontaneity, her disarming honesty) but also prepares the way for the tension between her world of human value and the world of material things, so cherished by her sister Vera and her sister's husband, Berg. Vera describes herself as "brought up differently" from Natasha; more strictly, in fact, according to her mother. The old Countess says that while Vera has suffered from too little freedom, Natasha may have been spoiled by too much (JI 9: 52). The first scene of the Rostovs' name-day party develops into a real conflict when Vera maliciously disrupts the harmless play of Natasha, Boris, Sonya, and Nikolay, thus isolating herself further from their world of warmth and intimacy. In this scene, Vera is already linked with Berg, himself an outsider, for Natasha says to her, "We don't bother you and Berg"—and indeed Berg removes Vera completely from the rest of the Rostovs (JI 9: 55).

Tolstoy clearly feels contempt for Berg and always describes him with great irony:

> In the war in Finland, also, Berg had succeeded in distinguishing himself. He had picked up a fragment of a grenade, by which an adjutant had been killed close to the commander-in-chief, and had carried this fragment to his commander . . . he talked to everyone at such length and with such persistency about this incident that people ended by believing that this, too, was something that had to

be done, and Berg received two decorations for the Finnish war.
[JI 10: 185]

So that Berg, whom Tolstoy treats so malignantly, describes Natasha as "utterly different, and her character is disagreeable, and
she has none of that intelligence like Vera's, but something, you
know . . . I don't like" (JI 10: 186). Tolstoy clearly intends that
Natasha be admired precisely for what Berg disapproves of and cannot understand in her.

These vignettes prepare for the climactic scene between Berg and
Natasha when Moscow is about to be abandoned and wounded
Russian soldiers are quartered in the Rostovs' home. Berg rushes
in and, in response to the count's queries about the situation, pronounces a long series of pompous platitudes about the army and
progress of the war. But this is not what Berg has come for; at a
time of national loss, death, and disaster, Berg has come to inquire
about using one of the wounded to help him move a bureau and
dressing table for Vera.

Natasha's merciless eyes had, upon his entrance, exposed Berg's
pretended concern for the crisis at hand: "Natasha stared at Berg,
as though seeking the solution of some problem in his face, and her
eyes disturbed him." And further on: " 'Altogether, the heroism
shown by the Russian soldiers is beyond praise, and beyond description!' said Berg, looking at Natasha; and as though wishing to
placate her, he smiled in response to her persistent stare . . ."
(JI 11: 314). But Natasha has sensed the truth, and although she
cannot articulate what she senses, her actions speak for her. Berg
wants to use the wounded, Natasha rushes to save them. In this
scene, Tolstoy states through Natasha his contempt for the petty
and materialistic and his reverence for human life.

The abundance of Natasha's nature, beautifully portrayed and
genuinely valued by Tolstoy, is an integral part of her womanhood.

On the other hand, her energy often appears excessive, and colors her behavior with wildness, even recklessness. This is suggested when Natasha first appears. At the name-day party she runs to her mother and stops short: "She had evidently bounded so far by mistake, unable to stop in her flight" (JI 9: 47). Natasha cannot control her passionate nature and unintentionally goes "too far." The same day, at the Rostovs' formal name-day dinner, Natasha, on a self-imposed dare, stands up at her place and impertinently shouts out, "What's for dessert today?" In reply, Marya Dmitriyevna calls Natasha a "Cossack"—which only provokes her to repeat the question. In a later scene, warned by her motherly feeling, the old Countess Rostov feels apprehensive that there is "too much" of something in Natasha, and that it will prevent her from being happy.

When channeled creatively, Natasha's abundant vitality, the "too much" in her, enlivens and restores the people around her. Again, her first appearance suggests this, as she infects the name-day guests with her spontaneous laughter: "She sank on her mother's lap, and broke into such a loud peal of laughter that everyone, even the prim visitor, could not help laughing too" (JI 9: 47). Later, the ball scene illustrates the undirected nature of Natasha's love: it is primarily an effusion of energy that she neither intends nor can avoid: "Natasha fell in love the moment she walked into the ballroom. She was not in love with any one in particular, but with everyone. She was in love with whomever she looked at for the moment she was looking at him" (JI 10: 48).

Pierre, too, is affected by Natasha's loving energy. At the Rostovs' name-day dinner, sitting opposite Pierre, Natasha gazes rapturously at Boris: "This gaze sometimes strayed to Pierre, and the look on the face of the funny, excited little girl made him want to laugh himself, though he didn't know why" (JI 9: 75). But the role that she plays in Pierre's life is not so much restorative as broadening, for he has his own kind of vitality. From Natasha, Pierre seems to draw new meaning and new possibilities in life, even though he cannot precisely define them.

If anyone is restored to life by Natasha, it is above all Andrey. Less accessible to even casual personal contact than Pierre, forever cut off from full involvement by walls of self-analysis and pride, Andrey needs Natasha's quick responsiveness and warmth more than any person who knows her. In one of the drafts, he says quite plainly of Natasha: "I love this playfulness and youthfulness; it makes me feel alive" (JI 13:691).

In the final version, Natasha's effect on Andrey is more subtly dramatized in his oft-noted visit to the Rostovs at Otradnoe. Suffering from moral and emotional anesthesia, "dreading nothing and desiring nothing," Andrey is surprised on seeing Natasha that the whole world is not infected with the same kind of *ennui:* " 'What is she thinking about,' he wonders, 'and why is she so happy?' " (JI 10:154). Later, Natasha's joy in the beautiful moonlit night gives Andrey a totally new perspective on his psychic state and pulls him out of his self-absorption. Miraculously restored to the living, Andrey leaves Otradnoe newly convinced that "life is not over at thirty-one" (JI 10:157).

Again, at the ball, exhausted by tedious political and intellectual discussions, Andrey feels "full of life and youth again" (JI 10:203) as he whirls Natasha around the ballroom. When Andrey's and Natasha's feeling for each other has later been tacitly recognized by everyone, Andrey talks freely to Pierre about what she means to him. Everything he says refers literally or metaphorically to the resurgence of life he feels from her: "I have never lived till now," he says. And for him, where Natasha is, "there all is happiness, hope and light" (JI 10:220–21).

But, though the power of Natasha's love has helped to overcome the inertia that locked him within himself, Andrey dies. He is destined to succumb; throughout *War and Peace* the Bolkonskys' world of intense, but heatless, passion is posed against the Rostovs' world of warmth and simplicity. When Andrey first visits as her suitor, Natasha herself tells her mother, "Only I'm afraid with him, I'm always afraid with him. What does that mean?" (JI 10:218). Later, we are told that "there had been a feeling of awkwardness in the family in regard to Prince Andrey. He seemed a man from another world . . ." (JI 10:227). The sense of Andrey's being somehow alien to the Rostovs is further deepened by Nikolay's reaction to Natasha's engagement: "Natasha was even-tempered, serene, and quite as light-hearted as ever. This made Nikolay wonder, and look on the engagement to Bolkonsky rather skeptically. He could not believe that her fate was now sealed, especially since he had never seen her with Prince Andrey. It still seemed to him that there was something not right in this proposed marriage" (JI 10:240).

Most telling, however, is the thought about Andrey which occurs to Natasha at her uncle's after the hunt. In response to Nikolay's half-joking reply to his uncle about choosing a husband for Natasha, she thinks: "What did Nikolay's smile mean when he said: 'One has been picked out already.' Was he glad of it, or not glad? He seeemed to think my Bolkonsky would not approve, would not understand our gaiety now. No, he would quite understand it" (JI 10:240). Even though Natasha is probably right about Andrey's understanding her uncle's way of life, Andrey's inherent reserve would keep him from actually participating in it, as the Rostovs are capable of doing.

Ironically, the same reckless quality in Natasha's nature that leads her to betray him and plan an elopement with Anatole Kuragin has human value for Andrey: through his anger, she makes him feel for the first time in his life the reality of love. When Andrey's late wife had flirted with other men in the salons of society, Andrey only looked on with cold disdain, always perfectly in control. But Natasha's fling attacks his viscera and he feels real pain.

Furthermore, Natasha needs forgiveness for this act, which was painful and confusing to her also, and she thus provides the occasion for him to overcome his pride. Before the battle of Borodino, Andrey recalls Natasha: "I understood her and more than understood her: that spiritual force, that sincerity, that openness of soul, the very soul of her, which seemed bound up with her body, it was the very soul that I loved in her . . ." (JI 11:212). Although he feels her betrayal intensely, Andrey is not so blinded by hurt pride that he distorts her real worth. Her need helps him to discover the humanizing power of forgiveness, even at the point of death.

Natasha, however, is not portrayed without ambivalence. Indeed, if one assumes that Tolstoy's attitude toward women was basically hostile, she could not be. Moreover, what he feared in Natasha (and in women in general) was not simply normal human weaknesses and failures; that is, by portraying Natasha ambivalently he is not merely making a believable human being. Rather he is expressing his fear of the very vitality that he simultaneously prizes in Natasha (and later, in Anna Karenina). For her vitality, indeed, any woman's, derives in part from her sexuality, a force that Tolstoy perceived as essentially destructive, particularly in women. His treatment of her in the Epilogue, where he in fact neutralizes the qualities associated with her sexuality—passion, warmth, quick responsiveness—will be discussed later.

Even prior to the Epilogue, however, we see in Natasha a destructive streak that coexists with her creative energies. Indeed, for Tolstoy the two seem inseparable. It is this destructive energy, clearly connected to sexuality, which, when she believes herself to be in love with Anatole, makes Natasha say, "Then I will be ruined; I will. I'll hasten to my ruin" (JI 10:347). Her words echo the demand for romantic love and self-destruction uttered by Masha in *Family Happiness.*

Natasha is at best a creature of grace and light; the Kuragins are creatures of the dark, and her innocence is highlighted against the dim background of their depravity. This is most strikingly apparent

in Tolstoy's comparison of Ellen Kuragin and Natasha at the ball:
"Natasha's bare neck and arms were thin and not beautiful. Compared to Ellen's shoulders, her shoulders were thin, her bosom unde-
fined, her arms thin. Ellen seemed to be covered with a varnish from
all the thousands of glances that had scanned her body, while Natasha seemed like a young girl stripped for the first time, who would
have been greatly ashamed if she had not been assured by everyone
that it must be so" (JI 10: 347). The implications of the contrast between Petersburg and Moscow are significant also in the intimacy
between Natasha and the Kuragins. After the ball, Audrey recalls
Natasha's "newness": "There's something fresh in her, original,
unlike Petersburg" (JI 10: 205).

The central episode of Natasha's plunge into the Kuragin world
is of course her brief but intense "affair" with Anatole Kuragin.
Why is it that she plots to run away with Anatole if, when she first
becomes involved with the Kuragins, Natasha is in love with and
engaged to Andrey Bolkonsky, one of the best matches in Russia?
Natasha "was as much in love with her betrothed, as untroubled in
her love, and as receptive to all the joys of life as ever." Yet, in
spite of her happiness, there is something that threatens Natasha's
peace: ". . . toward the end of the fourth month of their separation
she began to suffer moments of sadness which she could not fight.
She felt sorry for herself, sorry that all this time should be wasted
and be of no use to anyone, while she felt herself so able to love and
be loved" (JI 10: 271–72). Natasha's uneasiness is a symptom not
only of self-pity, but also of Andrey's own failure to commit himself
fully to her. He does, after all, submit to his father's imposing a
year-long waiting period before the wedding can take place, as an
attempt to forestall the marriage. After six months have elapsed,
Andrey writes to his sister that "I need nothing from [my father]. I
have been, and always shall be, independent; but to act in opposi-
tion to his will, to incur his anger when he has perhaps not long
left to be with us, would destroy half my happiness" (JI 10: 234).

Of course Andrey *does* want something from his father—permission to marry immediately—and, in fact, he is *not* independent. He refuses to resist his father's tyranny.

The crisis over "family" sharpens the psychic and emotional distance between Natasha and Andrey, particularly after her humiliating visit to the Bolkonskys at their home in Petersburg. Prince Nikolay Andreyevich refuses to see the Rostovs. But, in dressing gown and night cap, he manages to get a good look at Natasha without formally receiving her. And Princess Marya, envious of Natasha's charm and of her intimacy with her brother, can barely bring herself to make polite conversation. Natasha, in her turn confused and angered by their treatment, withdraws into herself and acts unnaturally. Against the ascetic background of Bolkonsky reserve, Natasha's exuberance and spontaneity falter and, worst of all, she becomes painfully self-conscious.

The scene renders Natasha more susceptible to the seductive flattery offered by the Kuragins. In one of the draft versions describing her first encounter with Anatole, Tolstoy describes Natasha as a "beauty ripened for love" (*sozrevšaja dlja ljubvi krasavica*) (JI 13:825). In the finished novel, she meets him in the fullness of her feeling for Andrey, wanting simply "to embrace the man she loved, and to speak and hear from him the words of love, which filled her heart" (JI 10:32). The man she loves, however, is abroad in order to improve his "health" and to placate an angry father. These pressures influence Natasha's mood just before she goes off to the opera.

In his caricature of the opera, Tolstoy creates a counterpart to Natasha's adventure with Anatole and to the romantic intrigues of society in general. At first Natasha responds to the opera characteristically; mildly repelled by its artificiality, she cannot grasp its meaning.

> She knew what it all was meant to represent; but it was all so grotesquely false and unnatural that she felt alternately ashamed and

amused at the actors. She looked about her at the faces of the spectators, seeking in them signs of the same irony and bewilderment which she was feeling herself. But all the faces were watching what was passing on the stage, and expressed nothing but an affected—so Natasha thought—ecstasy. [JI 10: 324]

To Tolstoy, the opera is pure contrivance. But the cardboard scenery, strange costumes, and artificial relationships reflect the corresponding artificiality in the society to which it is addressed. The distinction between performer and spectator is lost and Natasha herself becomes infected by this strange phenomenon:

> Natasha began gradually to pass into a state of intoxication she had not experienced for a long while. She lost all sense of what she was and where she was and what was happening before her eyes. She gazed and dreamed, and the strangest ideas flashed unexpectedly and disconnectedly into her mind. [JI 10: 325]

Ellen is very much the *prima donna* of this world that Natasha suddenly feels herself drawn to. To such an extent is Natasha under the spell of Ellen's self-confident sexuality that she actually begins to imitate her: "Ellen sat in her nakedness close to Natasha and smiled on all alike, and just such a smile Natasha bestowed on Boris" (JI 10: 326). Throughout the book, Ellen's carnivorous smile signifies something brutally sensual. A note in one of Tolstoy's journals may illuminate the meaning of that smile: "A beautiful woman smiles," he wrote, "and we think that because she smiles, she is expressing something good and true. But often the smile means something entirely foul" (JI 53: 73). And when Natasha imitates Ellen's smile, it means that something in her has responded to Ellen's world.

For Tolstoy, Natasha's response represents moral problems that concern not only Natasha but his general views of women. On the most immediate and personal level, Natasha's involvement with the Kuragins leads her to betrayal. She plans to break off with Andrey and run away with Anatole, who has engineered a phony "wedding." Natasha, of course, does not *know* Anatole; she sees him for a total of two or three times. But like Pierre with Ellen, she is completely intoxicated with the Kuragin sexual mystique. When she talked with Anatole for the first time at the opera,

> he never took his smiling eyes off Natasha's face, her neck, her bare arms. Natasha knew beyond all doubt that he was fascinated by her. That pleased her, yet she felt for some reason constrained and oppressed in his presence. When she was not looking at him she felt that he was looking at her shoulders, and she could not help trying to catch his eye to force him to look into her face. But as she looked into his eyes, she felt with horror that, between him and her there was not that barrier of modest reserve she had always been conscious of between herself and other men. She did not know how —but in five minutes she had come awfully close to this man. [JI 10: 329]

The recognition of "no barriers" is an ominous moment in the relations between Tolstoy's men and women.[4] It usually means strong mutual sexual attraction. It is that which tempts Masha of *Family Happiness* to throw herself "headlong into the abyss of forbidden delights" with the Italian marquis who pursues her. And Pierre feels the same in his relations with Ellen which precede and parallel Natasha's with Anatole.

Ellen's sexuality is brilliantly captured by Tolstoy in the famous salon scene which opens the novel:

> With a slight rustle of her white ball-dress trimmed with greenery, with a gleam of white shoulders, glossy hair, and sparkling diamonds, she made her way between the men who stood back to let her pass; and not looking at anyone in particular but smiling on everyone as if graciously affording each the privilege of admiring her beautiful figure, the shapely shoulders, back and bosom, which

4. See chap. 5.

the fashionable gown fully displayed, she approached Anna Pavlovna
as if she carried the glitter of the ball within herself. [JI 9: 14]

From this passage we can readily see why Napoleon refers to
Ellen as *"un animal superbe"* (JI 13: 685). But with all her beauty,
Ellen does not wish to please others so much as she seeks to please
herself. She is her own audience and the motive for her performance is self-love: "The princess leaned her bare plump arm on
a little table and did not think it necessary to say anything. She
smiled and waited . . . she sat upright, glancing occasionally first
at her beautiful rounded arm elegantly resting on the table, then
at her still more beautiful bosom on which she readjusted a dia-
mond necklace" (JI 9: 14). There is no warmth in Ellen's beauty
precisely because her entire identity is centered in a body which
Tolstoy both loves and fears. His love makes it beautiful, but his
fear makes it somehow impersonal and nonhuman. For her kind of
beauty, Tolstoy repeatedly uses adjectives like "marble" and "statu-
esque," attributes which point up the cold and inanimate quality
of Ellen herself. She is a consumer of admiration: every glance
serves as fuel to feed her vanity and to brighten the glow of her
enticing body.

Later at Anna Pavlovna's, Ellen's glamour traps Pierre and
convinces him that she "must become his wife":

> Her bosom, which always reminded Pierre of marble, was so close
> to him that his shortsighted eyes could not but perceive the living
> charm of her neck and shoulders so near to his lips that he need
> only stoop a little to have touched them. He sensed the warmth of
> her body, the faint breath of perfume, and the slight creak of her
> corset as she moved. He saw not the harmony of her marble beauty
> and her gown, but all the fascination of her body veiled only by her
> clothes. [JI 9: 249]

And, as with Masha and the marquis, and Natasha and Anatole,
between Pierre and Ellen "there existed no barrier now save the
barrier of his own will" (JI 9: 250).

Already overcome by Ellen's sexual power, Pierre is further trapped by the cosmopolitan society in which she moves and which is congenial to that sexuality. Just before Ellen's and Pierre's "betrothal," the intoxication of Prince Vasily's dinner clouds Pierre's sensibilities: "He had no clear vision or hearing, no understanding of anything. Only now and then disconnected ideas and impressions from the world of reality flashed through his mind" (JI 9: 256). Natasha's experience at the opera is similar when she is first attracted to Anatole: "She lost all sense of who and where she was and of what was going on before her. As she gazed and dreamed, the strangest fancies flashed unexpectedly and disconnectedly into her mind" (JI 10: 325). Clearly, Tolstoy is asserting that the Kuragins' radiant sexuality has the power to hypnotize and bewitch basically innocent people like Natasha and Pierre.

But in spite of all her dazzling beauty, Ellen makes Pierre uneasy and vaguely embarrassed about his decision to marry her. He feels that there is something more than dangerous about her—there is also something "foul, something forbidden" in their relations. Pierre recalls hearing rumors about incest between Ellen and Anatole, he reflects on the dubious reputation of the rest of her family—Ippolit and Prince Vasily. All of this causes him to feel that there would be "something vile and unnatural in this marriage," even "dishonorable," "obviously wrong," "not what he ought to do" (JI 9: 251). But simultaneously, from another part of his imagination, Pierre sees Ellen's image "in all its womanly beauty" (JI 9: 251), and he is once again overpowered.

In a society which has reserved sexual initiative exclusively for the male, Ellen usurps the male prerogative: she is openly aggressive in expressing her sexual appetite. This is particularly apparent in the scene directly following Prince Vasily's acceptance of the proposal which Pierre characteristically never quite made. In flustered relief that at last the whole matter is settled without definitive action on his own part, Pierre tries to remember what is said on such occasions, then bends to kiss Ellen's hand, "but with a quick rough movement of her head she met his lips and pressed them with her own. Pierre was struck by the transformed, unpleasantly distorted expression of her face" (JI 9: 259).

After his duel with Dolokhov, when Pierre has been thoroughly repelled by his marriage and wants to break off with Ellen, he sees clearly how he was trapped and hates himself for it:

> He suddenly had a vision of *her* as she was at those moments when he had most violently expressed his insincere love for her, and he felt the blood rush to his heart, and had to jump up again and move about and break and tear to pieces whatever his hands came across. "Why did I say to her 'I love you'?" he kept asking himself. [JI 10: 29]

Pierre's original hesitation and doubt, his early concern about Ellen's character develop into a deep sense of her immorality and hatred for his sexual involvement with her. Though proud of her "social tact" and "majestic beauty," he now sees only the depravity of her relations with Anatole, her coarse refusal to bear his (Pierre's) children, even the vulgarity of her speech: "How often, when thinking about her character, I have told myself that I was to blame for not understanding her, for not understanding that impervious composure and complacency and the absence of all preferences and desires, and the key to the whole riddle lies in the terrible word, depravity: she is a depraved woman. I have uttered the terrible word to myself, everything has become clear" (JI 10: 28). When Natasha meets Anatole and is attracted to him romantically and sexually as Pierre was to Ellen, she is spared the full circle of events that ends in disaster for Pierre. But not before she gets into serious trouble.

The sources of Natasha's attraction to Anatole can, of course, be traced in part to Andrey's absence and to his family's cruel rejection of her. But this is only part of the story; the rest centers around Tolstoy's fear of the very qualities which make Natasha one of Russia's favorite heroines—her free spirit, her independent judgment, her capacity for joy, her susceptibility to her own feelings. These are gifts that Natasha perverts when she plans to run away with Anatole. When uncontrolled, these passions—for life, happiness, pleasure—become, in Tolstoy's view, destructive, and fall outside rational control.

One remarkable passage of *War and Peace* dramatizes this dark side of Natasha's nature. At the close of the hunt scene with Nikolay and her uncle, ". . . Natasha, without taking a breath, gave vent to her delight and excitement in a shriek so shrill that it set everyone's ears ringing. In that shriek she expressed just what the others were expressing by talking all at once. And her shriek was so strange that she would have been ashamed of it and the others would have been surprised on any other occasion" (JI 10: 260). Merejkowski interprets Natasha's shriek as a "devilish" cry, primitive, and amoral.[5] Of course Tolstoy more than once connects "devilish powers" with women. In his short story "The Devil," the mysterious erotic forces embodied in a woman destroy a man who would otherwise have led a respectable and productive life. And Kitty of *Anna Karenina* feels that "there is something strange, devilish (*besovskoe*), and enchanting about Anna" (JI 18: 89).

Yet, while he ascribed to women devilish and subhuman powers, at the same time Tolstoy held them responsible to a conventional moral code. And because Natasha is herself demonic when her sexual vitality overflows beyond her control, it was not simple for Tolstoy to define his attitude toward her and the issues raised in the Kuragin affair. This episode, described by Tolstoy as central to *War and Peace,* was forged out of numerous draft versions. In some, Natasha is the unwilling victim of the Kuragin mystique, or of her own curiosity, or even of her immaturity—all of these are suggested in the final text. Anatole, on the other hand, receives the

5. Merejkowski, *Tolstoi as Man and Artist,* p. 208.

same treatment in the drafts as in the final version. He is characterized as completely amoral, a cad, but a guiltless cad: "Anatole
was incapable of considering how his actions might be considered
by others, or what might be the result of this or that action on his
part" (JI 10: 333).

In Pierre's judgments of Natasha, which vacillate in the drafts
from harsh condemnation to total forgiveness, one sees Tolstoy the
fox at his best. It was difficult for him to take a definitive stand
precisely because all postures were both present and possible to him.
Various drafts, summarized here, indicate the range of Tolstoy's
attitudes (all are from JI 13):

> Pierre explains to Natasha's father that the whole matter was
> a passing fancy, hits Anatole, and tells him ". . . you're not worth
> her little finger, do you understand?" (856)
> Sonya tells Pierre about the affair and at dinner at the Rostovs
> he "was silent and stared persistently and malevolently at Natasha.
> It seemed to him that he hated her." (857)
> Pierre orders Anatole to leave. (858)
> Pierre confronts Anatole and feels "that he had no right to in-
> terfere in this affair, that Anatole was right, that everything was
> so brief and so stupid."
> "No, he's not guilty," thought Pierre. "But poor Andrey, and
> that worthless, vile girl." (859–60)
> Sonya tells Pierre, who hits Anatole. "Pierre, who has argued
> with Prince Andrey against the impossibility of ever forgiving a
> fallen woman, did not ever ask himself if he would or would not
> forgive Natasha." (861)
> Pierre feels sorry for Natasha because she was capable of falling
> in love with a man whom he despises. The incident makes him
> feel the insignificance of everything and he "hated Natasha."
> "Anatole is right," he thought, "she is guilty and he is right."
> (865)

But, face to face with Natasha, Pierre softens and understands
that she was not guilty but only "sick." (862–63)

Pierre is in doubt but feels that Natasha was such an "elevated,
heavenly creature, who had given her love to the best man in the
world, Prince Andrey, and Anatole was such a stupid, crude, de-
vious animal." (866–67)

Pierre is tender and sympathetic with Natasha to the point of
adopting a "deferential tone." Andrey shows Pierre his letter from
Natasha: "You told me that I was free and to write you if I fell in
love. I have fallen in love with another. Forgive me. N. Rostov."
(867–69)

Tolstoy writes: "It was obvious that this letter was written in a
moment of moral sickness, and its laconic crudity was the more
forgivable for it, but more oppressive." Finally, Pierre asks Andrey
to forgive Natasha. (869)

In the final draft, Tolstoy's attitude is forgiving and indulgent. But
Natasha pays a price for her recklessness. Confronted with the two
Natashas, Tolstoy mutes the wild sensual Natasha, takes away the
primitive power which she displayed in her dance at her uncle's,
and transforms this "heavenly creature" into the model mother and
wife of the epilogue.

One of the literary stratagems for Natasha's redemption is her
eventual intimacy with and dependence upon Princess Marya. Indeed, after Masha has joined the Rostovs just before Andrey's
death, Natasha rarely appears without her quietly hovering nearby.
Tolstoy deliberately makes no attempt to distinguish and individual-
ize their reactions to Andrey's death: "After Prince Andrey's death,
Natasha and Masha *both alike* felt this. . . . *they* closed *their* eyes
. . . *they* guarded *their* open wounds. . . . Only alone *together* were
they safe . . ." (JI 12: 171, my emphasis).

Even Natasha's marriage is negotiated by Masha. When Pierre
sees that he must marry Natasha, it is to Masha that he first applies:

"But what am I to do?" he says. She replies: "Leave the matter to me. I know. . . ." Later in the same conversation, she says: "Write to her parents. And leave it to me. I will tell her when it is possible. I want this to happen. And I have a feeling in my heart that it will" (JI 12: 227–28).

As mediator, Masha imitates one of the traditional functions of the Virgin whose name she bears. But that is not her most important role in Natasha's development. Masha is essentially a self-effacing, ascetic woman, who lacks completely the sexual dimension that threatens Natasha's tranquil passage into marriage and motherhood. As such, Masha serves to neutralize Natasha's sexuality and assures a chaste apprenticeship for her future.

In the Epilogue to *War and Peace,* that future is flawlessly realized. We see a "new" Natasha, a thoroughly domesticated creature; to use Tolstoy's own metaphor, a breeding fish (*samka*). She and Pierre have been married for seven years and have four children. They are visiting Nikolay and Masha Rostov at Otradnoe, the Rostovs' old country estate, which is now flourishing under Nikolay's management. Overflowing with wives, husbands, children, tutors, nurses, and guests, the old house exudes an almost suffocating sense of "family."

Within this domestic scene, the central figure is, of course, Natasha. She is all the more striking in that she is barely recognizable. One must view this change, however, both as a further development of a familiar character acting within a continuing fictional context, but even more as a schematic figure whose function has become didactic. The basic theme of this portrayal is Natasha's complete devotion to family life: "The subject in which Natasha was completely absorbed was her family, that is, her husband, whom she had to treat so that he should belong entirely to her and to the home, and the children whom she had to carry, to bear, to nurse and bring up" (JI 12: 171). The exclusive concern with the care and comfort of husband and family leaves Natasha once again with little concern for her own inner and private life or for the outside world.

One consequence of this indifference is Natasha's physical appearance. Unlike the sleek Natasha who fussed impatiently over herself, Sonya, and her mother before a ball, she pays no attention whatsoever to her dress, hair, or figure. In fact, the "new" Natasha, broadbeamed and straggly haired, resembles a peasant woman. Tolstoy provides an explanation:

> Natasha did not follow the golden rule preached by so many clever people, especially the French, which says that a girl should not let herself go when she marries, should not neglect her accomplishments. . . . Natasha was no longer concerned about manners or speech, or her clothes. . . . She felt that the tricks instinct had taught her to use before would now seem merely ridiculous in the eyes of her husband. . . . She felt that the bond between them depended not on the romantic feelings which had attracted him to her but on something else as indefinable but as firm as the bond between her own body and soul. [JI 12: 171]

Natasha has forsaken not only her personal grooming but her social life as well:

> Society saw little of the young Countess Bezukhov, and those who did see her weren't pleased with her. She was neither charming nor amiable. It was not that Natasha liked solitude . . . but with her pregnancies, her confinements, the nursing of her children, and sharing every moment of her husband's life, she had demands enough, which could only be fulfilled by renouncing society. [JI 12: 266]

Renouncing society is, in Tolstoy's view, a positive act, particularly for a woman; from the opening scene in Anna Pavlovna's salon he depicts the salons and balls of society with irony and contempt. As in *Family Happiness,* for a woman to forsake home and family for teas and operas is to abandon her true vocation and opens the way to disaster.

WOMEN IN TOLSTOY 68

In the Epilogue, contemporary "discussions" on the rights of women and the relations of husband and wife are briefly mentioned but are given no serious consideration. To the contrary, Tolstoy makes it clear that Natasha is not only uninterested, but "had absolutely no comprehension" of those issues. He dismisses the entire controversy by avowing that "those questions, then as now, existed only for those who see nothing in marriage but the pleasure married people may derive from one another—who see only the first beginnings of a marriage and not all its significance, which lies in the family" (JI 12: 268). The Epilogue could indeed serve as a kind of marriage manual. In it are described the roles, functions, behavior, and ideal qualities of husband and wife. In order to make his point, Tolstoy draws a parallel between marriage and food. He argues that just as the purpose of food is nourishment, so the purpose and whole significance of marriage is the family. A brief period of "enjoyment" is allowed married couples, but it is limited to the "initial stages" of marriage. Tolstoy extends this metaphor in order to advocate monogamy. If the purpose of food is nourishment, he argues, then one eats only what is necessary—one dinner, instead of two or three —because the body can digest only one dinner (JI 12: 268). In like manner, only one husband and one wife are necessary to the family. Both *gourmets* and *gourmands* could happily refute any argument based on this particular analogy.

In spite of the generally positive view of marriage presented in the Epilogue, there are some aspects of the relationships of the Rostovs and Bolkonskys which are not completely satisfactory. In no way do these defects seriously flaw the general aura of solidity and loving peace that surrounds those families, but they are of some concern, particularly to the women of the family.

Masha, for example, just like the Masha of *Family Happiness,* thinks of Nikolay's work as an important part of his life that is inaccessible to her and the children—"she felt he had a world apart,

which he loved passionately, governed by laws she had not fath-
omed." [6] And though Nikolay's work is something Tolstoy generally approved of—farming the land, gaining the respect and support
of his serfs, improving his estate—one does feel that Nikolay is
rather more limited in his interests and passions than could be good
for anyone. His nephew, Nikolinka Bolkonsky, has a keen sense of
Rostov's philistinism in comparing him with Pierre: "He [the
nephew] did not want to be a hussar or a Knight of St. George like
his uncle Nikolay; he wanted to be learned, wise, and good like
Pierre" (JI 12:274). In addition, for all Rostov's concern and talent
for his work, he cannot avoid a suggestion of self-pity: "And then
there are you and the children [he says to his wife] and our affairs.
Is it for my own pleasure that I work on the estate or in the office
from morning till night? No, I know I must work to be a comfort
to my mother, to repay you, and not to leave the children such
paupers as I was left myself" (JI 12:289).

Masha silently rejects this attitude of Nikolay's but allows him to
think she approves and supports his ideas. Her other-worldliness, her
religious and spiritual cast of character, so different from Nikolay's
earth-bound practicality, focus all her energies upon what is right and
good for the children to do and know (an approach to the world
that characterizes her throughout the book). It is to Nikolay's
credit that he is deeply aware of Masha's special gifts which he does
not share and, far from resenting them, rejoices in them:

> This constant, tireless spiritual effort, the sole aim of which was the
> children's moral welfare, enchanted him. If Nikolay could have ana-
> lysed his feelings he would have found that his proud, tender,
> strong love for his wife rested on this very feeling of awe at her
> spirituality, at the lofty moral world, almost beyond his reach, in
> which she always lived.
>
> He was proud that she was so wise, and he fully recognized his

6. This is similar to Masha's feelings about her husband's world in *Family
Happiness*.

own insignificance beside her in the spiritual sense, and rejoiced all the more that a soul like that not only belonged to him but was part of his very self. [JI 12: 287]

It would be hard to find fault with this tender picture of a loving couple, yet in relation to their children one is disappointed to find no significant role for the father. Insofar as Tolstoy gives us an idea of the father's contribution to family life (he never specifically describes it, whereas he describes the mother's in great detail) it includes the worthy but vague imperatives to provide material well-being, love, support, and play. All this Nikolay does admirably, but to Masha, as to all good Tolstoyan mothers, is entrusted the spiritual and moral development of the family. In this area, Masha surpasses even Natasha, and approaches the Tolstoyan ideal.

As far as Natasha's marriage is concerned, the internal conditions of it show the consequences of Tolstoy's views of women and their place in the home. It is clear from the Epilogue that Natasha and Masha are in character, if not in influence, stronger and more vital than their husbands. Yet, while he gives these women a good deal of power in their own sphere, he warns us against its potential abuse. One cannot help but feel uncomfortable when Pierre is described as "in fact, henpecked (*pod bašmakom*)" (JI 12: 268). It would be irrelevant to posit contemporary sensibilities as primary in this reaction. Twentieth-century Americans constantly ruminate about the problem of matriarchy and the strengthened role of the mother at the expense of the central role of the father. But the resentment of the contemporary male implicit in this view is lacking in the Epilogue: "Pierre had been greatly surprised at his wife's view, to him a totally novel idea, that every moment of his life belonged to her and the home. His wife's demands astonished him but flattered him and he submitted" (JI 12: 269). Those demands are all-embracing: Pierre is not to drink, go to his club, pay attention to other women, spend money, or be away from home except with permission; but "to make up for this, Pierre was perfectly free to regulate life at home as he chose, for himself and his family." But this is a dubious compensation, for Natasha tries to follow Pierre's expressed wishes only as she understands them—a dangerous habit for any spouse. Even if Pierre wants to change his mind about something, Natasha meets him "with his own arguments" (JI 12:269). In other words, Pierre is head of the family by default: he is both allowed to have his way and deprived of the right to express it and to change it.

Most probably there is a good deal of wishful thinking on the author's part when he says of Natasha that "in her own home she acted like a slave to her husband, and the whole household went on tip toe when he was occupied. . . . Pierre had only to show his inclination to find his desire instantly being fulfilled. He had only to express a wish and Natasha would jump up and perform it" (JI 12:269). Natasha does allow him to pursue his intellectual interests but not if he spends longer at them than she thinks necessary—witness her anger and depression when he is away in Petersburg for longer than the agreed-upon time. If Pierre wants to discuss his political activities in Petersburg with the other men of the house, it is Natasha who arranges the conversation and smooths the way to further talk in case of disagreement.

These small tyrannies of Natasha's are presented as both innocent and necessary to her household, and far from causing Pierre any grief, he seems to thrive under her discipline. This is directly connected to Tolstoy's therapeutic view of marriage. He felt that marriage for both husband and wife provides an effective control over socially frivolous impulses and aimless eroticism. Pierre, in giving up flirting with women, dining with the boys at the club, drinking and carousing, has abandoned the dissipated and aimless life of the Russian aristocrat which Pozdnyshev describes in *The Kreutzer Sonata* and which Tolstoy himself led as a youth in Petersburg.

Marriage "saves" Natasha, too—from a world of salon chatter, women's rights, and the dark, frivolous world of the Kuragins. In this respect Natasha's experience contrasts sharply with that of Masha in *Family Happiness*. Natasha's ebullient nature, whose double edge leads her at once to both personal generosity and reckless abandon, finds focus and discipline in her love for Pierre and in the routines of children and home. For Masha (in *Family Happiness*) on the other hand, marriage is a centrifugal influence: it signals the onset of frustration, fills her with the urge to move outward from her husband and her children, and finally provides a desolate refuge from her inability to understand herself or to cope with her life. Thus Tolstoy presents two directions for marriage: it can lead to disintegration and disillusion (as for Sergey and Masha) or it can happily open the way to moral and emotional discipline (as for the Bezukhovs).

One is distinctly aware of the dangerous implications, however, of Tolstoy's "perfect" marriage. According to his portrayal, it seems that in order to maintain tranquility and working order as husband and wife both must lose themselves in the other and forsake their own identities, including their sexual identification as man and woman. In the Epilogue Tolstoy strips Natasha of her individuality and presses her into the familiar mold of demanding wife and concerned mother. Pierre is not much better off. Of him, Tolstoy writes that "after seven years of married life Pierre felt a firm and joyful conviction that he was not a bad fellow, and he felt this way because he saw himself reflected in his wife. In himself he felt the good and bad mixed and obscuring one another. But in his wife he saw reflected only what was truly good, everything not quite good was left out" (JI 12:270). After Pierre's long and painful search for self-knowledge and a philosophy of life, he does not find a satisfying identity in and of himself but relies almost entirely on his wife's opinion of him. Furthermore, "he felt that his way of life was determined now, once and for all, till death, and that to alter it was not in his power . . ." (JI 12:275). One wonders if this is the life promised by the comet of 1812 to Pierre, whom Natasha had then inspired with such hopes for the future. Or has his urge to know and act been totally defeated by Natasha's suffocating desire to have him all to herself and the family? Private experience in this case has totally supplanted public life and gives a special importance to the place of women in this novel. For whatever reasons Tolstoy was pessimistic about political activity and what it could accomplish, one would only believe from the Epilogue that Pierre's interest in his new movement of "joining hands" against corrupt government is purely a hobby, one that he would not have time to pursue seriously because of his family duties. Early in the book, Prince Andrey warned Pierre not to marry:

> But tie yourself up with a woman and like a chained convict you lose all your freedom! And all the hope and strength there is in you is only a burden to you and tortures you with regret. . . . If you only could know what these society ladies, indeed women in general, are! My father is right. Egoism, vanity, stupidity, triviality in everything—that's what women are like when they show themselves as they really are. When you see them in society, it seems that they might have something, but there is nothing, nothing, nothing! No, don't marry, my dear fellow, don't marry! [JI 9: 35]

Pierre in fact becomes the victim of that terrifying "family egoism" which only women feel, according to Tolstoy, and for which the whole world may perish as long as the family remains intact.[7]

Tolstoy presents in the Epilogue a bizarre theory of marital equilibrium: the role of the individual man or woman acting on the demands of will, conscience, or passions, is lost as one mate absorbs the other and as both are consumed by the family. In the absorption of the individual into the family, Tolstoy is in fact striving toward the selfless ideal of life most characteristic of his late period, but present even in the young Tolstoy. His diary of 1852, fourteen years before the completion of *War and Peace,* contains the

7. Gol'denvejzer, *Vblizi Tolstogo,* p. 54.

following plan for a novel: "The hero seeks in country life the realization of an ideal of happiness and justice. Not finding it, and disillusioned, he would seek it in family life. But a friend suggests that
happiness lies not in an ideal, but in the constant lifelong effort
which has the happiness of others as its goal" (JI 46: 146).

So that, although Tolstoy viewed this marriage in the Epilogue
with approval and enthusiasm, the happy resolution of *War and
Peace* for Natasha and Pierre is not a thoroughly satisfying one.
It is, in fact, only one of a double image, the second of which Tolstoy was compelled to expose in his greatest and most complex
treatment of marriage: *Anna Karenina.*

Anna Karenina: A Fragile Equilibrium

> And his attitude toward women . . . is one of implac-
> able hostility. There is nothing he likes so much as to
> punish them—unless they are just ordinary women like
> Kitty and Natasha Rostov. Is it the revenge of a man
> who has not achieved as much happiness as he is capable
> of, or the hostility of the spirit toward the "humiliating
> impulses of the flesh?" Whatever it is, it is hostility, and
> very bitter, as in *Anna Karenina.*
>
> Gorky

The writing of *War and Peace* extended to four years, but it
was relatively free of the conflict that accompanied almost every
stage of the writing of *Anna Karenina.* Although the initial idea of
Anna Karenina occurred to Tolstoy in 1870, he began work on it
only in 1873, wrote sporadically for the next four years, and finished
the last part in 1877. These passages from two letters in 1876 and
1877 to the editor and critic Strakhov illustrate his often contradictory feelings about the writing and the content of *Anna Karenina:*

> I loathe what I have written. The galleys of *Anna Karenina* for the
> April issue of *Russkij Vestnik* now lie on my table, and I really
> don't have the heart to correct them. Everything in them is so rot-
> ten, and the whole thing should be rewritten—all that has been
> printed too—scrapped, and melted down, thrown away, renounced;
> I ought to say: I'm sorry, I won't do it any more; and try to write
> something fresh instead of all this incoherent, neither fish-nor-fowl-
> ish stuff. [1876, JI 62: 265]

I must confess that I was delighted by the success of the last part of *Anna Karenina*. I had by no means expected it, and to tell you the truth I was amazed that people should be pleased by something so ordinary and insignificant. [1877, JI 62: 307–8]

These remarks could reflect the chronic dissatisfaction with their work that most great writers, Tolstoy among them, usually feel. Yet his contradictory feelings about the thematic content of the novel posed a real obstacle to unraveling its many threads and did, eventually, frustrate its resolution. Furthermore, *Anna* was a final work of its type, for Tolstoy did "renounce" it, along with all his belles lettres that predated the *Confession* written only three years after *Anna* was completed. It is clear that *Anna Karenina* was written during a painful period of crisis.

We know that Tolstoy's original intention was to portray his heroine-adulteress as "pitiful" (*žalkaja*) rather than "guilty" (*vinovataja*). That deceptively simple notion inspired the complex moral and literary development of the finished product. The centrality of the book is certain: Tolstoy felt that *Anna Karenina* could help to elucidate all his fictional characters and themes precedent to it.[1]

Although *Anna Karenina* will continue to disturb and baffle its readers, a passage from Tolstoy's introduction to his *Recollections* can be used as a conceptual model for an interpretation of this perplexing novel. In that passage, Tolstoy divided his life into four periods. The first, according to him, was his "innocent, joyful, poetic childhood up to fourteen." Then came the "terrible twenty years that followed—a period of vulgar profligacy, devoted to ambition, vanity, and, above all, lust." He describes the next as the "eighteen-year period from my marriage to my spiritual birth—which from a worldly point of view could be called moral. That is, during those eighteen years I lived a correct, honest, family life, not practicing

1. N. Gudzij in his "Istoria pisanija i pečatanija 'Anny Kareninoj'" (JI 20: 57) discusses Tolstoy's feelings about the centrality of *Anna Karenina*.

any vices condemned by social opinion. But all the interests of that period were limited by selfish concerns for my family, increasing our property, attaining literary success, and pleasures of all kinds." Finally he entered the fourth, twenty-year period in which he was still living and in which, he writes, "I hope to die, from the standpoint of which I see the meaning of my past life, and which I should not wish to change in any way except for the effects of the evil habits to which I grew accustomed in the former periods." (JI 34:347).

Tolstoy meant these four periods to describe his moral development, but they correspond roughly to his artistic development as well. Within these four phases, the line of continuity is not perfect; for example, the fiction that best illustrates his "second period"— most notably *The Kreutzer Sonata*—was not written during that period, but very late in life. Also, this periodization, described from the bitter perspective of Tolstoy's seventy-fourth year, was imperfect: again, the second period focuses on his sexual adventures at the expense of his equally demanding quest during that period for romantic love and an ideal mate. Regardless of the distortions of Tolstoy's later perspective, these four periods nonetheless represent the layers of motives and dilemmas present in all of Tolstoy's fiction, though at any given moment one or another may predominate.

The range and quality of experience in this fourfold model, moreover, provide the content and the artistry of *Anna Karenina*. For *Anna Karenina* is not a book with a single theme, but many themes. We can easily assume that Tolstoy wanted to recapitulate for himself and for his readers everything that he knew about men, women, and life before he moved to his final attempt to renounce what he knew and return, if possible, to something like that "innocent, joyful, poetic childhood." In this great summing-up, however, there is no catharsis, no resolution. For just as Anna's despair intensified but distorted her sensibilities just before her suicide, the edge of crisis and conversion sharpened and deepened Tolstoy's already comprehensive vision of life. And because Tolstoy was morally and artistically no longer capable of simplifying that vision, the many themes of *Anna Karenina* resist resolution and coexist only in a fragile equilibrium.

Tolstoy's first sketches of Anna herself show a stereotyped image of a wayward woman: she is loud, vulgar, and shallow (JI 20). One cannot imagine for her the complex fate which awaited the real Anna. Yet this initial conception is interesting precisely because the stereotype is not a human being but a moral attitude, even a prejudice, which at first overpowered Tolstoy's human intention to create a sympathetic character. The Anna that finally emerged is not only a sympathetic character but a captivating one as well. Her beauty and elegance, her vitality, her instinctive tact, her warmth— these are all qualities that were characteristic of Natasha Rostov, and like Natasha, Anna readily engages the moral and aesthetic affection of the reader. But Anna is a much more powerful character, for hers are the richer, and more dangerous, energies of a mature woman; moreover, a woman who is not quite happy.

Anna is introduced, ironically enough, as a mediator, summoned to the Oblonsky household to repair the damage that her brother's affair with his children's governess has created. The dramatic function of the context in which Anna is introduced is twofold: it foreshadows, of course, the demolition of her own household and, indeed, her entire life.[2] Beyond that, however, Anna, Stiva, Dolly, Vronsky, and all the other characters of these opening pages are introduced as people in whose environment adultery is an assumed form of experience. It can be painful, and disruptive, to be sure, but it is as much a part of their expectations and ambiance as mar-

2. V. Šklovskij in "Parelleli u Tolstogo," *Xod Konja* (Berlin, 1923), p. 124, points out Tolstoy's use of kinship (*rodstvo*) and its related technique of "escalation" (*stupenčatost'*) that could very well apply here. He says that just as Nikolay Rostov was a "simplification" of Natasha, so Stiva reveals one aspect of Anna's character. He is a "step" toward the understanding of her much more complex character.

riage or theater or politics. In these opening pages Tolstoy plunges the reader *in medias res* and does not really offer relief from the constant reality or threat of disruption and chaos throughout the rest of the novel.

Yet, in her role as peacemaker, Anna initially seems to be protected against this threat. "My sister Anna will be here tomorrow," Stiva announces to his valet Matvey. "Thank God," Matvey answers. Both men somehow assume that Anna is the kind of person who can make everything "turn out right." We expect, therefore, a woman of good, strong character, whose family life is equally strong and tranquil. But Matvey then asks a question which dimly alludes to the possibility of a skeleton in Anna's closet (to which she herself will later refer): "Is she coming by herself or with her husband?" (JI 18:7). His question suggests that her husband's presence would in some way alter Anna's behavior, obstruct her mission, or at least, affect those qualities of hers most needed to effect a return to normalcy.

One of those qualities is Anna's warmth and animation; the abundance of her vitality associates her, like Natasha, with an attachment to life and to the things that maintain and restore life. Yet there is also a suggestion, as there is in Natasha, of a dark side to this exuberance. When Vronsky first sees Anna at the train station, he is immediately attracted by the "restrained animation of her face"; she seems to overflow with "something that against her will expressed itself now in the sparkle of her eyes, now in her barely perceptible smile" (JI 18:66).

Why "against her will," why "barely perceptible"? This passage suggests of Anna's inner life that she is aware of her own sexual appeal, that she consciously desires to control it, and that she may unconsciously desire romance. Quite early in the novel, we learn that she is deprived of life and love with Karenin in that sense. When Dolly recalls a visit to the Karenins' home, she remembers that "she had not liked their house; there was something false in the whole atmosphere of their family life" (JI 18:71). And when Dolly compliments Anna at the end of her trip on the serenity and goodness of her heart, Anna replies mysteriously that there is a "skeleton" in her closet, too, and that it is a "gloomy" one indeed (JI 18:104). The vagueness of her remarks implies that she herself probably does not know specifically what she means.

Yet when Anna meets Vronsky it is she who makes the first flirtatious move. He responds quickly, but she draws back, not wanting "to continue the conversation in that tone" (JI 18:68). Vronsky pursues Anna, however, by way of his awkward visit to the Oblonsky house on the night of her arrival. His pretext is to find out the details of a dinner date there, but upon seeing Anna a look of "shame and fear" appears on his face, while she feels at once pleased and apprehensive (JI 18:81). Kitty assumes that Vronsky has come to see her, a delusion that is cruelly exposed at the ball, where Anna completely captivates Vronsky, whose proposal Kitty had expected at any moment.

In a way, Kitty had innocently challenged Anna. Entranced with this beautiful older woman, vaguely aware of the power of her sexuality, and perhaps unconsciously wanting to disarm her, Kitty tells Anna that she pictures her at the ball in innocent lilac. Smiling, Anna replies: "Why must it be lilac?" (JI 18:78)—that is, "What makes you think I'm *that* kind of woman!" At the ball, however, "Anna was not in lilac as Kitty so much wanted her to be, but in a low-necked black velvet dress. It exposed her full shoulders and bosom which seemed carved out of old ivory and her rounded arms with the very small, delicate hands" (JI 18:84). Contrary to what she had expected, Kitty sees something bewitching and devilish (*besovskoe*), even cruel, about Anna's beauty and charm (JI 18:89). Indeed, the exposure of Anna's shoulders and bosom and their ivory color immediately conjure up the image of Ellen Kuragin, whose sexuality captures and imprisons Pierre Bezukhov. Anna's charisma is more potent, however, because its source is not only the sensuality of her body, but of her spirit as well.

Though Anna's initial attraction to Vronsky is consciously against her will, in conversation with Dolly after the ball she admits that it may have been "a little bit" her fault, that perhaps she did something "against her will" to make Kitty's evening a disaster and spoil her hopes of a proposal from Vronsky (JI 18: 104–5). Because Anna feels guilty about and threatened by her feelings for Vronsky, and guilty for having made an enemy of Kitty, she wants to hurry away from Moscow back to the familiarity and safety of Petersburg. When she settles herself on the train, she thinks: "Thank heaven tomorrow I shall see Seryozha and Alexey, and my life, my nice, ordinary life will go on as before" (JI 18: 106).

In these first episodes, Anna is already portrayed ambivalently. With the Oblonskys she performs her duty well; with real love and concern for the continuity of their family life, she asks Dolly to forgive Stiva and resume her duties as wife and mother. She romps with their children who adore her. With delicate maternal feeling, Anna displays photographs of her son. Escaping from a potential affair with a dashing young officer to the quiet safety of her own family, Anna is the very model of wifely, motherly, and social virtues. Yet when she reaches her destination, her son does not seem to be as appealing as before, and Karenin promises nothing beyond his habitual pomposity. And Vronsky, having declared his passion, is with her, never to leave her again.

The beginning of Anna's affair with Vronsky poses two questions: how did such a woman come to marry a man like Karenin, and why does she fall in love with Vronsky? A partial answer to these questions can be found within what might be called Tolstoy's sociology of marriage, for the patterns of falling in love and marrying in the novel combine both his personal attitudes and the habits of his culture.

Falling in love in Tolstoy's fiction is at best an apparently simplified and idealized process. The potential lovers recognize each other instantly, understand each other intuitively, and are conscious of a shared commitment. Beyond this, however, and in contradiction to it, lies Tolstoy's basically more cynical belief that men and women cannot know each other, and are ignorant of and vulnerable to their individual limitations. Although Tolstoy was extraordinarily sensitive and "modern" in defining and portraying this problem, the twentieth-century notion of communication is not meant here. Perhaps nineteenth-century men and women did have to rely solely on the explicit exchange of trivialities and the implicit communication of feeling that mean falling in love for Tolstoy. This treatment of falling in love, however, is not so much expressive of his concern for a faulty psycho-cultural practice as his dismissal of, and even contempt for, a better alternative.

For Anna and Vronsky, their exchange prior to the consummation of their affair consists almost entirely of polite chit-chat and meaningful looks exchanged at social rendezvous. These can be, admittedly, perfectly effective ways to express oneself, but they have finally to do more with maintaining private illusions than with revealing oneself or the discovery of another. Of course, Vronsky's declaration to Anna on the train trip back to Petersburg is vividly direct, but it is a single dramatic encounter, an announcement rather than a revelation.

It is the same with Kitty and Levin. When they meet and talk at Stiva's dinner party long after Kitty's initial refusal of Levin, he rejoices that "there was apparently nothing extraordinary in what she had said, but what inexpressible meaning there was in every sound of her words, in every movement of her lips, eyes, and hands as she said it!" (JI 18: 405).

The perfect example of this wordless communication is the alphabet game that Kitty and Levin play that same evening (a supposedly autobiographical detail). Levin writes, "w, y, t, m, i, c, n, b, d, y, m, n, o, o, t?" and Kitty correctly fills in the right words, "When you told me it could not be, did you mean never or only then?" (JI 18:418). This episode is meant to illustrate the total, intuitive understanding which exists between people who love each other even before they themselves realize it. Its presence need only be tested by some kind of game. A similar test appears in *Family Happiness* when Sergey Mikhailych cloaks his proposal of marriage in the self-derisive story of "A," the old man, who foolishly falls in love with "B," a lovely young girl. In that case, too, Masha rises like Kitty to the challenge, defends their relations, and overcomes her lover's uncertainty.

These ritualistic tests and games show Tolstoy groping beyond sentimentality toward a statement of the essentially ludic dimension of falling in love—the ambitious and often decisive games of lovers. Always present in romantic love as he sees it, this ludic element is central in the affairs of fashionable men and women.[3] For them such games are elegant and trifling pastimes used to dispel boredom and to formalize their relations. In addition, the men and women of *Anna Karenina* think they are in love—and actually marry—for the equally formalized demands of honor, social or financial advantage, and family tradition. Karenin, we know, proposed because Anna's aunt managed to make him feel that he had "compromised" Anna, that is, had been courteous to her on more than one occasion. Princess Shcherbatsky, too, felt that Vronsky was surely going to propose to Kitty for the same reason. And, indeed, according to *her* code, the one which governed her own marriage, "there could be no doubt whatever about the seriousness of his intention" (JI 18:48).

The old princess is not sure how to manage Kitty's future: should she make a unilateral decision and arrange the whole matter for her daughter or should she allow Kitty complete freedom? In tra-

3. The classical treatment of this subject is, of course. J. Huizinga's *Homo Ludens* (Boston: Beacon Press, 1964).

ditional Russian style, the Shcherbatskys' own marriage was arranged by a matchmaker. Yet the mother is both aware and afraid
of the new freedom for women (who attend the university and "go
out alone") in their relations with men. To her mind, such freedom
is as safe as "loaded pistols" for children (JI 18:49). So that, although both tyranny and permissiveness are unacceptable, the princess's society does not offer a compromise strategy that can preserve
the "reputation" of her daughter.

Her sense of helplessness encourages the old princess, and indeed
all of her society, to seek refuge in the conventions, which, although
they promise comfort and respectability, conspire to produce superficiality and deep confusion of feeling. That is, just as Tolstoy says
about Karenin's work that he deals only in the "reflections" of life,
so does his entire society deal only in the reflections of passion and
commitment.

Kitty and Levin represent the very best that these conventions
offer; their relations, in fact, are a youthful version of the dignified,
decent, and comfortable marriage of their parents. As previously
discussed in Chapter 2, their wedding ceremony, described at length
and in great detail, is impeccably correct and set the tone for their
life together. The care and detail lavished upon the description of
their wedding creates and corresponds to the solidity with which
Levin and Kitty are established in a love and marriage that begin
in a thoroughly conventional manner. The symbolic value of this
traditional Moscow wedding places them in the direct tradition of
the Russian country gentry which Tolstoy was later to deride. Simultaneously, the Levins provide sharp contrast to the bohemian, illicit
affairs of society and the self-involved romantic passion of Anna and
Vronsky.

If the Levins' marriage represents the best that social conventions
can produce, the affairs of Betsy Tverskoy's *haut monde* are the
eccentric products of rebellion within those conventions. For in
Anna Karenina, the stylization of behavior and feeling permits

equally the appearance of respectability and the betrayal of public morality. In order to protect both goals, Betsy and her friends willingly practice hypocrisy and deceit. During Anna's "cosy chat" with Betsy on the day after the races, Anna presses Betsy for details about a certain society affair. Betsy replies that "in good society people do not talk or even think about certain details of the toilette" and the same applies to their romances (JI 18:314). Even for Anna, "lying, so alien to her nature, had become not merely simple and natural in society, but even gave her satisfaction" (JI 18:312). This perverted sense of satisfaction is turned against Karenin himself, when he notes about his disgrace that "they all seemed elated, just as though they had come from a wedding. When they met him, they asked after his wife's health with barely concealed glee" (JI 18:442). This glee is a corruption of the ludic quality, the human instinct for play, that is more innocently expressed in games like Levin's and Kitty's.

In addition to a pretense of decency or the corrupt passion for play, Betsy's appeal to Anna to restrain her curiosity reveals the vested interest of class. The entire novel is dotted with the liaisons of aristocrats with ballerinas, actresses, and peasants (as in Voslovsky's and Oblonsky's interlude during their hunting trip with Levin). Revealing the minutiae of these interclass adventures is perfectly permissible; Betsy encourages Vronsky to relate every detail of his efforts to make peace with the titular councilor, Venden, whose wife is pursued to her door by his fellow-officers. The smooth operation of the *beau monde* is somehow too fragile to absorb criticism and humor with tranquility. (Betsy, we are told, seldom laughs.) But both can be easily applied to the life of a lower class. By virtue of this displacement, the self-adulation and the self-assurance of the aristocratic elite can survive unruffled.

The "graceful" liaison with a married woman which Vronsky's mother would welcome as the final accreditation of his social success epitomizes the elegant model of adultery cherished by high so-

ciety (JI 18:184). Yet Countess Vronsky and her peers eventually
ostracize Anna and Vronsky because they betray the only style of
romantic love which had interest and excitement for them: it must
be chic, clandestine, schizophrenic. Though all of these apply in
some degree to Anna and Vronsky, they are (mortally) serious
about their love, even to the point of parodying the convention
which to society signifies only boredom and frustration: they live
together, have a child, manage an estate. For Betsy, the bonds of
marriage can be properly ignored only if they are preserved intact as
a background for infidelity or an object of mockery. Thus her society, bound by its own rigid conventions, is not equipped to deal
with the semi-legitimate, semi-underground nature of Anna's affair.
In Vronsky's own words, "if it had been an ordinary, banal society
affair, they would have let me alone. But they feel that it is something different, that it's not just a game, that this woman is dearer
to me than life. And this is incomprehensible and therefore annoys
them" (JI 18:193).

In her desire for this experience of real love, Anna embraces the
fate that Masha both wanted and feared in *Family Happiness;*
Vronsky is Anna's Italian marquis who brings her to the edge of
the abyss and fulfills her wish for romantic love. Masha's fear of
the abyss prevents her from surrendering to the marquis and eventually returns her to her family. In contrast, although Anna feels both
"dread and happiness" upon hearing Vronsky's declaration of love,
"there was nothing unpleasant or gloomy about that tension or the
fantasies which filled her imagination; on the contrary, there was
something joyful, radiant, and exhilarating in it" (JI 18:110). Wil-
liam Dean Howells wrote of *Anna Karenina* that "when you have
once read it you know how fatally miserable and essentially unhappy such a love must be." [4] But it is impossible to deny Anna's
genuine happiness with Vronsky and his true love for her. It is also

4. W. D. Howells, *My Literary Passions* (New York: Harper and Brothers,
1895), pp. 254–55.

impossible to overlook both Tolstoy's fascination with and attraction to their passion.

It is true that after her confession to Karenin Anna's vision of her future with Vronsky corresponds to Howells's view and anticipates an eventual reality: "She never would experience the freedom of love and would always remain the guilty wife, continually threatened with exposure, deceiving her husband for the sake of a shameful relationship with a man who remained independent and a stranger and whose life she could never share" (JI 18: 310). Before this vision becomes a reality, however, Anna and Vronsky are truly happy. Once settled in Italy, Anna's

> will to live . . . was so strong and the conditions of life were so new and so pleasant that Anna felt unpardonably happy. The more she got to know Vronsky, the more she loved him. She loved him for himself and for his love of her. To possess him completely was a constant joy to her. His intimacy with her was always a delight. All the traits of his character with which she was becoming more and more familiar were inexpressibly dear to her. His appearance . . . was as attractive to her as to a young girl in love for the first time. In everything he said, thought, and did, she saw something exceptionally majestic and noble. . . . He was more than ever affectionately considerate to her, and the thought that she must never be allowed to feel the awkwardness of her position never deserted him for a moment. [JI 19: 31–32]

Yet Tolstoy clearly suggests that the joy of their Italian interlude will in fact turn in upon itself and become "miserable" and "essentially unhappy." The absorption in themselves and each other proves almost suffocating to Anna: "The very intensity of [Vronsky's] solicitude for her, the atmosphere of care with which he surrounded her was occasionally a little too much for her." While for Vronsky, it is not enough: "For a while after joining his life with [Anna's] . . . he felt the delight of freedom in general . . . and the freedom of love, and he was content—but not for long. He soon became aware that there arose in his heart the desire for desires—boredom. . . . Sixteen hours of the day had to be filled somehow. . . ." Vronsky is, as Tolstoy observes in an editorial aside, the victim of the "eternal error men make in imagining that their happiness depends on the realization of their desires" (JI 19:32).

The pressures of Anna's self-enclosed world with Vronsky soon test and warp their romantic idyll. Even before Italy, when Anna and Vronsky meet after the races, her romantic fantasies of him are blemished by actuality: "As at every meeting with him, she blended the picture she had of him in her imagination (incomparably better than, and, indeed, quite impossible in reality) with him as he really was" (JI 18:376). (This recalls Anna's reaction to her son when she returns to him after her visit to the Oblonskys: "She had imagined him to be nicer than he actually was. She had to come down to earth to enjoy him as he was." [JI 18:114]) As for Vronsky, as the tension of the relationship builds, he observes Anna "as a man might look at a faded flower he had picked, in which he found it difficult to discover the beauty which made him pick and destroy it" (JI 18:378). For Levin, whose relation to Kitty represents at best his expansion of responsibility and humanity, love "saved him from despair and . . . the threat of despair made this love stronger and purer" (JI 19:75). Romantic love for Anna, in contrast, diminishes her world, constrains her human capacities, and finally focuses her attention exclusively upon herself.

To fill the hours of the day and the gulf that ever widens between their expectations and what they can actually offer each other, Anna and Vronsky turn to a series of pastimes. Vronsky dabbles in art, philanthropy, country politics, managing an "English" estate. But when Dolly visits that estate, regardless of her renewed affection for Anna and her genuine admiration of Vronsky, she is uncomfortable at the "general unnaturalness of grown-up people carrying on a children's game in the absence of children. . . . She felt as if she were acting in a theater with actors better than herself and that her own bad performance was spoiling the whole show" (JI 19: 211).

These "performances" represent Anna's and Vronsky's vain struggle to find a successful alternative to the artificial life they formerly led and the one they have created in its place. Because she cannot be the hostess in Vronsky's home, because she has no "wifely" duties, because she loses all interest in her little daughter, Anna turns to a pathetic succession of hobbies: reading, writing a children's book, fostering a young English girl. Their most dangerous pastime, however, becomes their cult of sexuality.

Anna's first sexual encounter with Vronsky is described in an elliptical style characteristic of Tolstoy only when he is writing about sex. Briefly and allusively, it presents a fragmentary and unappetizing picture of the consummation of their desire for one another:

> [Vronsky] felt what a murderer must feel when he looks at the body he has deprived of life. The body he had deprived of life was their love, the first stage of their love. There was something dreadful and repelling in the recollection of what had been gained at this terrible cost of shame. Shame at her spiritual nakedness crushed Anna and communicated itself to him. But in spite of the murderer's great horror before the body of his victim, that body had to be cut up and hidden, for the murderer must enjoy the fruits of his crime. [JI 18: 157–58]

This unappealing picture leaves no doubt that the capitulation to their sexual desire is seen, quite consistently, by Tolstoy as a tortured, murderous act. Furthermore, for Anna it initiates a painful schizophrenia—the same split that tortured Tolstoy when he indulged himself sexually while feeling the moral demand for restraint and self-denial.

Kitty and Levin, in contrast, try to reach beyond the humiliation of their first sexual experience:

They continue to recall their honeymoon, that is, the first month after their wedding from which Levin had been taught to expect so much, not as a time of tenderness, but as the most painful and humiliating time of their lives. They both tried later on to erase from their memories all the ugly, shameful circumstances of that unhealthy period when both were rarely in a normal state of mind and rarely quite themselves. [JI 19: 71]

Though their humiliation parallels Anna's and Vronsky's, Kitty and Levin have undergone before their first physical union a "sexual purification." Just before their wedding, Levin gives Kitty his diary, which includes his sexual biography; he wants her to read it and forgive him his "debauchery" of the past. In doing so, Levin celebrates a bizarre ritual, the source of which is sexual guilt and the object of which is absolution, the preparation of a moral *tabula rasa* before marriage.

There are three steps to this ritual: First, sexual misconduct is recognized and acknowledged, and contrition is felt. Though we are told nothing specific, Levin's sexual "sins of the past," of which he is ashamed, are alluded to early in the book. Next, with the handing over of the diary, this guilt is expressed and confessed. This step is extremely painful for Kitty, but essential to recognizing the full extent of Levin's misbehavior: "It was only when [Levin] called that evening before going to the theater, went into her room, and saw her sweet tear-stained pathetic face, the unhappiness caused by the irremediable sorrow he had caused, that he realized what a gulf separated his shameful past from her dovelike purity and was horrified by what he had done" (JI 18: 429). But with a reminder that what she has read is "dreadful," Kitty forgives Levin in the final step of this three-part episode. After contrition, confession, and absolution, Levin can forget his sexual guilt under the assumption that his sexual energies will express themselves no longer lasciviously—that is, aimlessly—but only with the purpose of creating a family. In addition, this *rite de passage* marks not just a promise of but a conversion to monogamy.

This is at least the conscious motive of the ritual. However, like any complex human act, particularly one in Tolstoy, it has implicit intentions as well. One can see in it the hostility toward women deeply felt by Tolstoy and existing just under the surface of all his writing. For it is hostility that combines with innocent braggadocio to help the man celebrate his masculinity and announce his sexual capacity to the woman. The record of sexual adventures also serves to remind the woman that the male is freer than she and can always return to his former habits if he is not happy at home. It is precisely this freedom in Vronsky's life—though he does not exploit it—that Anna comes to resent bitterly. So that the woman's outrage and pain, while giving release to the shame of the man, at the same time applauds his exploits and insures both her sexual compliance and her fidelity. When Valerya Arsenev, to whom Tolstoy almost became engaged, was reduced to tears by Tolstoy's diary, he later commented: "The more she cried, the better I felt." [5] If this interpretation is not overextended, Tolstoy's dichotomous view of woman as the embodiment of chastity and of eroticism is revealed in this ritual. For he invests the virgin bride with the priestly power of absolution while at the same time he prepares her to be a sexual mate.

As mentioned earlier, Levin's promise of monogamy bears with it a new and acceptable role for sexuality, the creation of a family, which contrasts sharply with the use of sexuality in Anna's life. Central to Tolstoy's notion of the family is that it disciplines, justifies, and redeems sexual relations. More than that, it places sex in a natural, biological order which can minimize its erotic and maximize its functional essence. The total demands of family within this scheme

5. The erratic course of Tolstoy's relationship with Valerya Arsenev is recorded in his diary of 1856, JI 47.

will then hopefully transform the selfish sexual urges of mother and father. This is the promise implicit in the final sentence of *Family Happiness*. Natasha, of all the characters discussed in these chapters, is most integrated into this natural ideal of the family; Kitty, is too, and especially Dolly, whose life contains little else. The awful burden and the joy of her children distract her from the misery of her marriage.

For Anna and Vronsky, who live together without the formal discipline of a legitimate marriage, the role of sexuality is not diminished; to the contrary, it becomes crucial, at least for Anna. She refines and limits her roles with Vronsky to the extent that she becomes solely a sexual companion. As she rides to the train toward suicide, her dreary complaints revolve around this very point: "If only I could be anything but his mistress, while passionately loving nothing but his caresses! But I can't and I don't want to be anything else!" (JI 19: 343).

Just before she starts out to the train station, she sees Dolly for the last time. Kitty is with Dolly, but does not want to greet Anna. Dolly persuades her, however, and Kitty's hostility swiftly changes to sympathy for the pathetic woman she finds, so different from the brilliantly successful Anna whom she had once admired and envied. Thoroughly distraught and resentful, Anna wants to make it clear to Kitty that Levin has not only visited her, but that she found him attractive: " 'He came to see me and I liked him very much,' she said with obvious ill will" (JI 19: 339). Her former reserve and discretion, and her embarrassment before Kitty, are replaced by arrogance and spite. She is no longer innocent in desire or purpose: "If I were an immoral woman," she thinks, "I could make her husband fall in love with me—if I wanted to. And I did want to" (JI 19: 340). Her aggressive wish to seduce is far different from her restraint with Vronsky in parallel episodes early in the book.

In their use of sexuality, according to Tolstoy, Anna and Vronsky stand at odds with nature. Kitty and Levin are in tune with their country life and experience humanly nature's perils and joys: decay, death, birth, rebirth. At the birth of his son, Levin feels a terrible awe before Kitty: "She suffered, complained, triumphed, and rejoiced in the suffering and loved it. He saw that something beautiful was taking place in her soul, but what? That he could not understand. That was beyond his comprehension" (JI 19:285–86). Instead of participating in this mystery, Anna more and more uses her physical mystique purely to attract and bind Vronsky. Her sexuality does not have "purpose" and finally she frankly refuses to have any more children. In her conversation with Dolly at Vronsky's country house she reminds Dolly: " 'You must realize that I am not his wife: he loves me as long as he is in love with me. And how else can I keep his love? Like this?' And she stretched her white arms out in front of her stomach" (JI 19:214). To Tolstoy, this is outright perversion, more abhorrent in a woman than in a man.

Anna's relation to the children she does have—her son, Seryozha, by Karenin, and her daughter, Anna, by Vronsky—is warped by her sense of guilt and despair. Although we can scarcely imagine Anna showing off a stained diaper, as Natasha does, Anna genuinely loves her son, and, at first, her little daughter too. Yet she finally denies the biological and institutional bond that ties her to her children in her attempt to combine sex with love.

Seryozha, in fact, is a constant reminder to both Anna and Vronsky of the impossibility of their life together. At two dramatic moments, he brings into focus a crisis in their affair. When Vronsky visits Anna before the races, their delicately furtive treatment of the child is a rehearsal of the hypocrisy which they have increasingly had to practice in society; this time, however, before an innocent person. The boy's confusion about their relations reflects their own: just before she was surprised in the garden by her lover, Anna asks, "Am I not my husband's wife?" (JI 18:198).

That is, Seryozha's hesitant and faintly hostile attitude to the two together makes especially Anna feel the acute pressure of her own divided conscience. As it grows more necessary for her to decide her course of action, she becomes paralyzed and vague. When she reflects on what Seryozha will think of her in the future, she "could not think, but, like a woman, tried only to calm herself with false arguments and words" (JI 18:200). And when Vronsky tries to talk to Anna about what they should do to resolve their situation, he encounters the same "superficiality" and frivolous judgment from Anna. But her vagueness and self-doubt help her to evade the "terrible guilt" which she feels before her husband. Unlike Tolstoy's heroes, Anna does not want nor is she able to face and solve her moral dilemma. She can only run away from it.

Seryozha is not only a real reminder of Anna's guilt, but also the obvious alternative to continuing her affair with Vronsky. In that same scene with Vronsky before the races, Anna describes their relationship. Comparing herself to a starving man, she says she may be cold, tattered, and ashamed, yet she is happy because she has food. "This is my happiness," she says. The next line begins, "She heard her son's voice"—once again calling her to another option (JI 18:201). The pressure which he innocently exerts on Anna to resume her responsibilities as wife and mother proves unbearable to her, and she flees with Vronsky to Italy.

Although this is a painful alternative for Anna, it is suggested even before that she will leave her son. Thinking over her situation, "she remembered that partly sincere, though greatly exaggerated, role of a mother living for her son which she had assumed during the last few years, and she felt with joy that in her position she had someone to hold on to, quite independent of her relationship with her husband and Vronsky. . . . Whatever position she might find herself in, she could not give up her son" (JI 18:305). But shortly after that, Anna realizes that should Vronsky ask her to run away with him, "she would give up her son" (JI 18:333). These passages suggest that Anna's attachment to Seryozha is part of her general

wish to love and be loved, to have something of her own, to be part
of life. These wishes, in turn, are more basic to her role as a romantic heroine than as a mother.

When Anna returns to Seryozha for the last time, he once again
serves to show Anna, this time, not the options available to her but
the consequences of the choice she has irrevocably made. The scene
is moving not only because of its real sadness and warmth, but
because Anna and her son are in a final relation to one another.
Her son no longer presents her with an alternative to Vronsky but
with the finality of her isolation. A furtive intruder in her son's
room, Anna knows she is lost to his world, her conclusive evidence
the gifts for Seryozha forgotten in her carriage.

The guilt that Anna feels as a result of abandoning her son
later corrodes her feelings toward little Anna. Though she is her
natural mother, Anna rejects the child totally. With the practiced
eye of a mother, Dolly realizes that Anna is a stranger to her baby's
nursery: when Anna wanted to give her daughter one of her toys,
she could not find it. Two extremes meet when Anna talks with
Dolly about not having any more children: she is completely alienated from her "natural" life and Dolly is completely a victim of it.
Yet Dolly finds some relief as a victim, while Anna is drawn ever
more toward a literal suicide.

It should be noted in passing that Vronsky, in contrast to Anna,
becomes increasingly attracted to the idea of family. Described in
the beginning as opposed to family life, he "regarded the family
and particularly the husband as something alien, hostile, and above
all, ridiculous" (JI 18:62). Yet he eventually wants desperately to
marry Anna, give *his* name to their daughter, and legitimize their
family life as much as possible. Given the attitudes toward adultery, divorce, and remarriage in Russia of the 1870s, it may have
been more perceptive of Anna to realize that that option was closed
to them. Vronsky's wish, in turn, may have been merely symptoma-
tic of his wanting to be *comme il faut*. But when he asks Dolly to

appeal to Anna to get a divorce and even speaks of the children they may have in the future, his request is genuinely touching and shows that he has grown.

Anna's refusal to be a wife to Vronsky and to bear more of his children parallels her larger estrangement from the whole world of women. In her exile, Anna is either alone or with men: "She sees no woman but Dolly," Stiva explains to Levin (JI 19: 272). And from the two opening paragraphs of *Anna,* it is evident that the woman, as wife and mother, plays the central role in preserving the family's unity and tranquility. During the Oblonskys' crisis, the harmonious relations of husband and wife are shattered, the family loses it cohesiveness, and everyone—children, tutors, servants—feels lost. Upon close examination, we see that this is not so much because of Stiva's adultery, but because Dolly has removed herself from the center of the household and is not performing her crucial duty of keeping the delicately balanced mechanism in running order. One distinctly feels that, had Dolly bravely kept silent about Stiva's affair and kept up her duties as head of the household, the adultery would have neither attracted attention nor resulted in disaster. After all, Anna appeals to Dolly to forgive and forget, not to Stiva to stop having affairs. As her affair with Vronsky begins, Anna too abdicates her role and finds herself eventually alienated from the precious kinship and approval of the sisterhood. In short, the community of women is united by the common roles assumed by each in her family.

At one point during the writing of *Anna Karenina,* Tolstoy (according to his wife's diary) glanced at the piping on his dressing gown and began to think about the whole world of women who concern themselves with such things. His musing culminated in the insight that because of her relations with Vronsky, Anna is cut off from her "own kind," the women who embroider, talk together about their lovers and families, and judge other women.[6] In the

6. Tolstaja, S. A., *Dnevniki 1860–1891* (1928), p. 36.

book there are really two feminine worlds, but to Tolstoy only one was truly feminine. Betsy's world is not a woman's world in the sense of a community of interests which center around the family and home. Quite to the contrary, her world is dedicated to holding such things in contempt. Kitty's world, on the other hand, is filled with *broderie anglaise,* preparing raspberry jam, discussing the virtues of various styles of diapers, cleaning house, all the thousands of domestic tasks that only her kind of woman considers necessary and natural. It is her world which, for Levin after his marriage "had assumed a new, hitherto unsuspected significance for him," and "now rose so high in his estimation that his imagination could not grasp it" (JI 19: 48). These women are the keepers of order, the time-honored goddesses of the hearth, whose special relation to life Levin envies, though not so much as to want to imitate it.

As her ties with Vronsky deepen, Anna is evermore attracted to Betsy's world and isolated from Kitty's and Dolly's. Because she no longer shares people, occupations, or passions with these women, she no longer shares even a common language with them. This is evident when Dolly comes to visit Anna at Vronsky's estate. Somehow they never get around to the "good talk" that Anna seems to anticipate so eagerly. Anna and Dolly have a long history of friendship but in this encounter they allow their roles to polarize and prevent them from talking honestly. Instead, they replace sincere discourse with the language of surface and subterfuge as each retreats defensively into her role, Dolly as *femme de ménage,* Anna as *femme fatale.*

Kitty's success in her world only emphasizes Anna's alienation. Later, when Anna bids a final farewell to Dolly, Kitty emerges triumphant from the nursery to greet a woman who has deserted a son and ignored a daughter. When she sees Kitty, Anna realizes that she is no longer in any "social" relation to anyone. Her isolation from her "own kind" is perhaps the greatest deprivation Tolstoy can imagine for her. One by one, as all other relations are stripped from her, Anna loses her private identity and her individual character. For Tolstoy, the loss of her "sociological" identity amounts to the loss of her personal identity as well.

The problem of moral judgment in *Anna Karenina* is, of course, the one most discussed and most elusive.[7] Had Tolstoy not prefixed to *Anna Karenina* the epigraph "Vengeance is mine, I will repay" (Rom. 12.19), the issue might have been easier to define and resolve. For that epigraph poses the possibility of revenge, or retribution for a crime or evil act committed by a guilty person. These questions, then, naturally follow: Who has done something wrong, what have they done, and who is seeking revenge? Yet one must be careful not to exaggerate the meaning of the epigraph or its power to clarify the moral issues in *Anna Karenina*. As Eikhenbaum has rightly argued, no novel, particularly one so large and complex as *Anna Karenina,* can be summed up or explained by its epigraph. And furthermore, *Anna Karenina* is not a novel of jurisprudence, designed as a mechanical exercise in the assignment of moral responsibility and the administration of justice. It is the artistic product of a sophisticated and humane imagination at the height of its powers. And that imagination turns in *Anna Karenina* to the problems of human feelings and responsibilities in conflict, not to questions of legality.

Two formal systems, civil law and orthodox religion, provide an institutional method for dealing with Anna's adulterous relations with Vronsky, her refusal to divorce, and her abandonment of her

7. It has been discussed by, among many others, Dostoevsky in the July–August 1877 issue of *Dnevnik pisatel'ja;* Aldanov, *Zagadka Tolstogo,* chaps. 3 and 4; Ejxenbaum, *Lev Tolstoj,* vol. 3, part III, chap. 3; and F. R. Leavis, *Anna Karenina and Other Essays* (London: Chatto and Windus, 1967). M. Gromeka's analysis (*Poslednie proizvedenija gr. L. N. Tolstogo*), to which Tolstoy gave his own stamp of approval, has been effectively dealt with and discounted by both Aldanov and Ejxenbaum, whose own discussions are so rewarding.

husband and family. But insofar as they both are the product of a
society which Tolstoy conceives of as hypocritical and corrupt, they
are treated with contempt and dismissed as invalid. When Karenin
goes to see the famous Petersburg lawyer about arranging for a
divorce, he notices in the lawyer's eyes that same *Schadenfreude*
that his friends and colleagues can scarcely conceal: "There was
triumph there and delight." He is struck, too, by the discrepancy
between the legal treatment of his case and his own conception of
it. While he considers adultery to be a serious breach of moral responsibility, Karenin finds that the law scarcely discriminates between it and desertion, or "physical defects of the mate" (JI 18: 387).
In describing the grounds for divorce, the lawyer adopts the tone of
a merchant selling pistols, "who after describing the advantages of
one kind of pistol over another, waits for his customer to make his
choice." But what is most repugnant to Karenin is the necessity for
his participation in the "detection of adultery by mutual agreement."
The lawyer patiently explains that divorce cases "fall under the juris-
diction of the ecclesiastical court, and the reverend fathers are keenly
interested in the most minute details" (JI 18: 388–89).

   This humiliating possibility does not merely shock Karenin's over-
developed sense of decorum, but penetrates beyond into genuine
moral indignation. The lawyer and the reverend fathers are request-
ing Karenin to stage-manage a performance of his own cuckoldry
in which Anna and Vronsky would portray the leading roles in
their own romantic tragedy. Far from determining the extent to
which the married partners have failed moral and divine law, the
law and the church, like society, demand mere contrivance, the
salacious acting out of immorality. The concerns of church and
state in this view are, like Karenin's, convention and the "reflections
of life" rather than the complexity of human feeling and the equita-
ble relief of pain. Legal procedures and formal religion, then, are
clearly not adequate to judge Anna or anyone else.

   Another faulty semi-religious judgment of Anna comes from

Countess Lidya Ivanovna, dowager queen of that group labeled the "Conscience of Petersburg Society" and whose women are described as "elderly, plain, virtuous, and religious." Though Anna at first maintained friendly relations with this circle, it gradually became unbearable to her, for "she had a feeling that she and all of them were acting a part, and she felt so bored and uncomfortable in that society that she visited Countess Lidya Ivanovna as little as possible" (JI 18:134). And, in fact, the first overt signs of social censure of Anna do come from the countess when we are told that she refuses to summer near the Karenins in the country. Not only does she ignore Anna, but to Karenin she also hints at Anna's relations with Vronsky. Naturally, as the "conscience" of Petersburg society, she would take a rigorous view of adultery.

But the countess is clearly a fool; her religious attitudes are cultish and lead her to deify such phony "mystics" as the Frenchman Landau, or Count Bezzubov, as he is absurdly rechristened in Russia. She pronounces pieties which she cannot practice: "There is no sin for a true believer," she says; "the sin has already been expiated" (JI 19:314). The countess herself, furthermore, feels more than friendly to Karenin. Though she herself would surely never admit it, she carries on a flirtation with him. So that not only is her self-righteous judgment of Anna corrupted by her hypocrisy, it is also in part motivated by her desire for closer relations with Karenin.

Levin, too, judges Anna. After he has visited her and returns home to Kitty, he feels that there was "something that was not quite right about the tender pity he felt for Anna" (JI 19:280). This feeling is more than a reflection of his talk with Oblonsky very early in the book. During that conversation, Levin confesses that for him, predictably enough, there are two kinds of women: "Or rather, no . . . there are women and there are . . . I have never seen and I don't think I shall ever see any charming fallen creatures, but women like that painted Frenchwoman . . . at the cashier's desk, the one with the curls, are an abomination to me and all fallen creatures are the same" (JI 18:45).

In response to this view, Stiva reminds Levin of the fallen women in the New Testament, hoping to evoke the Christian law by which Karenin himself felt compelled to forgive and love his enemies. Although Stiva was not able to soften Levin's attitude, real experience of Anna, who is both kinds of woman and more, did. Her beauty, her good taste, her charm, and the disarming simplicity with which she handled her difficult situation all conspire to engage not only Levin's admiration but his sympathy as well. Yet in spite of the elevated ethical view of life that he finally arrives at, that sympathy disturbs him. It was "inappropriate," Levin continues to believe, to visit a woman who could be described only as a "fallen woman." For his lofty notion of the "law of good and evil disclosed to mankind by revelation" is perhaps too high-minded to coexist with his conflicting reactions to Anna's personal appeal and her moral "fall." Levin is, moreover, painlessly unaware of the hypocrisy that allows both his concern over visiting a "fallen woman" and his lack of concern in continuing his friendship with Oblonsky, who is after all an habitual adulterer. A perfect case, in a word, of the double standard.

Least competent to judge Anna, however, is the very *beau monde* whose style of life Anna tries to assume. Its attitude is at first encouraging; Vronsky knew that there was

> no risk of his becoming ridiculous either in Betsy's eyes or in the eyes of all fashionable people. He knew perfectly well that in their eyes the role of a disappointed lover of a girl or of a single woman in general might be ridiculous. But the role of a man pursuing a married woman, who had made it the purpose of his life to draw her into an adulterous association at all cost—that role had something grand and beautiful about it and could never be ridiculous. [JI 18:136]

Vronsky's mother applauds the "graceful society liaison" (JI 18: 184) which she at first considers his pursuit of Anna to be. As Anna and Vronsky pass beyond the conventions of typical society affairs, however, Betsy and Vronsky's mother and all their friends become confused and finally vindictive. As Betsy warned Anna, "there is fashion and fashion, and there are ways and ways of rebelling" (JI 18: 314).

It has become a critical cliché to say that Anna is ostracized because she does not try to conceal her affair or because she takes it seriously. Such a judgment ignores the fact that society does not reject others (Oblonsky, Betsy herself) who also do not try to hide their extramarital relations. There is some truth, however, to the assertion that Anna is censured because she and Vronsky take their affair seriously. When Vronsky tries to "legitimize" their relations, by appealing to his friends to treat him and Anna as married, he is met with single-minded resistance. His affair with Anna has lost its public appeal and its new desperation is intolerable to a society which embodies and worships the pursuit of the trivial. Surely the "revenge" of society does not represent the "revenge" of the epigraph. For the *haut monde* in Tolstoy's *Anna Karenina* neither has moral principles nor is it subject to moral law: the greatest crime it can imagine is failure of style.

Although all of these judgments of Anna—religious, legal, personal, social—are finally flawed, there still remains the question of defining the central moral issue of the novel and Tolstoy's relation to it. If one reflects on the various conflicting positions that Pierre *in loco* Tolstoy took toward Natasha's betrayal of Andrey, one can imagine the problem Tolstoy faced in dealing with Anna, who betrayed not only her husband, but left her son and household as well. The question of his attitude is inextricably bound to his artistic conception of Anna.

Does Tolstoy succeed in portraying Anna as he had originally intended, as "pitiful" rather than "guilty"? In a way, Tolstoy's own ambivalence toward Anna helped him to achieve that humane portrayal of Anna which is, indeed, the success of the novel. For it is clear that, consciously, his own moral sympathy for Anna diminishes proportionately to her failure to live as he thought a woman should. Yet a deeper humanity, a surrender to Anna's mystery and even an identification with her sexual rebellion, finally protects Anna from the reader's, and Tolstoy's, censure. Though she may be "guilty" in many ways, Anna's fate is too complex to arrive at a secure final judgment.

In a letter to Strakhov (1876) Tolstoy relates that, as he was describing Vronsky's feelings after his interview with Karenin, much "to [his] amazement" Vronsky tries to shoot himself. Upon reflection, it appeared to Tolstoy that this attempted suicide was "organically necessary" for the further development of the novel (JI 62:269). This reflects the possibility that Anna too took on a literary life of her own, not subject to Tolstoy's preconceived notions of what she would do but which reflected what he thought she *had* to do.

When we speak of the "tragedy" of a literary character, we mean formally to evoke two tragic principles: one, that inner flaws and outer pressures conspire to destroy the hero or heroine; the second, that the hero or heroine willfully makes a series of conscious choices which logically and inevitably lead to disaster. Anna embodies and acts on both these principles. In a society whose feelings are both superficial and ephemeral, her wish to combine love, sex, and commitment makes her incapable of living within that society. Furthermore, like Masha of *Family Happiness,* Anna wants not to play at life but to experience it directly. She mistakenly believes that the "achievement of her desires" in romantic love will assure her happiness; but in Tolstoy's view, it can only guarantee her disillusion and isolation.

This inner demand for love and happiness is instinctive, part of Anna's nature; she, therefore, cannot control it or its consequences. Also beyond her control is that "mysterious force" which colludes with her own and Vronsky's limitations to confine and destroy them. It is that "harsh, mysterious force" which, Karenin believes, governs life and "demands the fulfillment of its decrees." Its symbol is the terrifying blizzard which engulfs Anna and Vronsky when, at the train station, Vronsky makes his confession of love to Anna. It is an immutable, nonrational logic of events which does not lead people to their destiny, but surrounds them, like amniotic fluid, as they themselves proceed to it.

But Anna herself conspires with this mysterious force by consciously choosing alternatives which can only lead to her death. These choices are influenced both by her own feeling of guilt and her "literary" conception of her fate. Whether or not the reader may judge Anna "guilty" she herself certainly does. When she reflects on her life she realizes that she "would always remain the guilty wife" (JI 18: 310). Her guilt is the source of her schizophrenic reaction to Karenin at the birth of her daughter: she clutches him to her with one hand and pushes him away with the other. She wants, in addition, to be punished for her guilt: "Oh, if I'd been in [Karenin's] place, I'd long ago have killed or torn to pieces a wife like me, and not have called her 'Anna, *ma chère*'" (JI 18: 379).

Incredulously she asks Vronsky if it is possible that they should one day be "like husband and wife, by ourselves, with our own family" (JI 18: 457). Yet she has refused the unconditional divorce that Karenin had offered: "Tell me yourself," he had said, "what would give you real happiness and peace of mind" (JI 18: 451–52). Caught between her desire for Vronsky and her guilt before her husband and son, Anna chooses not to choose and finally opts for purgatory, where, in Karenin's words, "ruin itself seems salvation to her" (JI 18: 415). One could say of Anna and Vronsky, as de Rougemont says of Tristan and Iseult, that "unawares, and passionately deceiving themselves, they have been seeking all the time simply to be redeemed and avenged for 'what they have suffered'—

the passion unloosed by the love-potion. In the innermost recesses of their hearts they have been obeying the fatal dictates of a wish for death; they have been in the throes of *the active passion of Darkness.*" [8]

This determination to suffer and to seek actively the fulfillment of an essentially literary style of life is similar to Masha's behavior discussed already in Chapter 2. In order to soften and evade the harsh realities of her position, Anna takes refuge in the role of Tragic Heroine. The part she plays is suggested by Betsy's warning to Anna that she is inclined to look at life "too tragically" (JI 18: 315). Liza Merkalov tells her that she is a real "heroine out of a novel" (JI 18: 314). Vronsky's mother accuses her of indulging in "desperate Werther-like passion" (JI 18: 184). When the disintegration of her life begins to accelerate, Anna herself stages the acts of her life, including seduction scenes with Vronsky: "While dressing, she paid more attention to her toilette . . . as if he could fall in love with her again because she wore the dress and did her hair in the style most becoming to her" (JI 19: 111).

Because Anna cannot attain real happiness either with her husband and son or with Vronsky, she substitutes a dramatic self-centered life of her own. The performance cannot last, however, just as all plays and all novels must end. Finally, Anna loses artistic control and her role-playing degenerates into a total and pathological abstraction from herself: "Who is that?" she asks, when she sees her feverish face with its glittering eyes reflected in a mirror (JI 19: 334). She takes morphine and finally opium—both of which reveal her passage into the world of hallucination and dementia. The question, then, of judgment and moral retribution in *Anna Karenina* is finally one that centers around Anna herself. She judges herself guilty, chooses to continue an impossible way of life, and

8. D. de Rougemont, *Love in the Western World,* tr. M. Belgion (New York: Pantheon, 1956), p. 46.

executes her own death sentence. When Anna throws herself under the wheels of the train, she both punishes herself and takes revenge on Vronsky and all the others whom she blames for her condition. But just as Levin felt that there was something "not quite right" in the pity he felt for Anna, so the reader is left with the uncomfortable feeling that the harsh verdict of the wheels is also "not quite right." That feeling derives from the fact that Tolstoy "allowed" Anna, one can only feel, to seek a conclusion, not a resolution, to her life. And not simply because any resolution that one could devise would inevitably be untenable, but rather because Tolstoy himself could not fully resolve the tension between Anna's personal charisma and her own morality.

Throughout the book, Tolstoy describes Anna as a woman of not only vital sexual power but of great personal warmth and natural grace of character. The language that evokes this image is at first elegant, characterized by restraint and balance. However, as Tolstoy's moral disapproval of Anna increases, so does his attraction to her, until his last descriptions of her become lush and irresistible. When Levin looks at Anna's portrait, he sees a "living, lovely woman with black, curly hair, bare shoulders and arms, and a wistful half smile on lips covered with soft down. She looked tenderly and triumphantly at him with eyes that disturbed him" (JI 19:273). The real Anna has the same "remarkable beauty which the artist had caught in the picture. . . . Yet there was something new and attractive about her which was not in the portrait" (JI 19:274). Disarmed by the power of Anna's sexual mystique, Levin cannot resist his own instincts and confesses to himself later that he "almost fell in love" with Anna.

Tolstoy's own attraction for and sympathy with Anna, which approach wanting to *be* Anna, are the more understandable when one considers the events in his own life that paralleled hers. For had he not himself become involved in an adulterous liaison, with Aksinya

Bazykin, the wife of one of his own peasants? [9] (The episode furnished the factual and thematic content of his story *The Devil*.) And had he not refused his responsibility toward the son that resulted from that relationship? The complexity of the moral issues involved in the whole of *Anna Karenina* extends far beyond this story in Tolstoy's own life. But it can help explain the source of Tolstoy's animosity toward Anna if it is seen as, in part, self-hatred, and her suicide as the exorcising of the "humiliating impulses of the flesh." His experience of genuineness in his relationship with Aksinya, the knowledge of his own guilt, and the dread of the consequences of his breach of responsibility find an artistic parallel in the inner forces that exact a heavy price from Anna Karenina, Tolstoy's most complicated heroine.

In yet another letter to Strakhov (1876), Tolstoy cites as the organizing principle of his works a mysterious "labyrinth of connection," the elemental life of which cannot be expressed in words and which must not be dissected for the sake of critical analysis. However elusive its nature to the writer himself, Tolstoy placed great value on the "linking principle" (*sceplenie*) of organic unity (JI 62: 268–69). Nowhere is such a principle more evident than in *Anna Karenina*, especially in the labyrinth of connections between men and women depicted there. The density and the variety of these peripheral connections, often only casual or briefly noted, constitute a typology, a fictional catalog of relations. Yet they are so skillfully deployed that they never submerge the principal figures and their stories, but serve only to illuminate and intensify them. Furthermore, this typology, like the main action itself, derives its life from the tensions implicit in the fourfold pattern of his life described by

9. Tolstoy's feelings about his relationship with Aksinya are most warmly reflected in his diary of 1858 (JI 48) when the affair began. His feelings of guilt toward her and toward his son by her, Timofej, are clearly expressed in a passage in his notebooks of 1909 (JI 57: 218).

Tolstoy in his *Recollections* and quoted at the beginning of this chapter. Within this typology, he explores the dimensions and the consequences of all the various possible bonds between men and women, in keeping with his view of *Anna Karenina* as a novel of summation.

There are Ivan Parmenov and his wife, newly married peasants working together in the fields in the full splendor of their "strong, newly awakened love." There are the solid, old-style Shcherbatskys, reminiscent of the old Rostovs. There is Levin's friend Sviyazhsky and his indulged wife. There are the strange, pathetic relations of Nikolay Levin and his mistress Marya Nikolayevna, and Koznyshev and Varenka. All of these differ, of course, from the frankly illicit society affairs which counter-convention turns into dangerous games: Prince Kaluzhsky and Liza Merkalov, Sappho Stolz and "Vaska"; the efficient Prince Chechensky, who takes his son to visit his illegitimate family because it "broadens his mind"; and, of course, *la femme la plus dépravée,* Betsy, adultery's muse.

Of these peripheral relations, only one approximates the innocence, joy, and poetry which Tolstoy assigned to the first period of his life: that of the Parmenovs, whom Levin somewhat enviously observes as they work together in perfect harmony. Though they are, of course, not children, they briefly represent the natural ideal of Tolstoy's childhood and are suggestive of the same concept of primitive purity represented by Maryanka of *The Cossacks*. In any case, the model of the four periods is not a device that can be mechanically applied to Tolstoy's fiction in perfectly consistent parallels, but should be more sensitively used as a model for qualities of experience that are juxtaposed.

In *Anna Karenina,* the specific world of children, for example, does not embody an innocent ideal of purity or joy, but is an aspect of the more or less legitimate human concerns of conventional family life. Anna's son Seryozha is a victim of the disruption of these concerns: he reflects and absorbs the chaos that results from the rupture of the "correct, honest, family life" which Tolstoy later described with so much contempt. Dolly's children, though she loves them dearly, are often a painful and maddening burden to her; she is frequently exasperated enough to call them "vile," "nasty," and "depraved" (JI 19:175). Though Levin's child reminds him and Kitty of the continuity of life at the moment of Nikolay's death, the baby's function in Levin's life is not so much personal as metaphysical, for he points toward some higher meaning that Levin cannot as yet comprehend.

Most of the major and the peripheral relationships described in *Anna Karenina* are illustrative of Tolstoy's second period. They reveal the "ambition, vanity, and, above all, lust" of a promiscuous and degenerate society. And despite their charm and the sympathy they inspire, Anna and Vronsky must reluctantly be placed in this category too. Their affair turns them in upon themselves and diminishes rather than expands their possibilities. Yet, though Tolstoy deliberately dismissed it from his periodization, Anna and Vronsky simultaneously represent the urge toward romantic love and the fulfillment of a perfect passion that both complemented and challenged the pure sexuality of that second period. It is this dimension of their relationship that is doomed to fail, not because of a moral law that demands revenge, not because of a treacherous society, not even because of their own personal limitations, but because Tolstoy continued in *Anna Karenina* to conceive of *eros* as debasing and self-destructive.

The fluidity and the integration of the "linking principle" in this novel are apparent in another aspect of Anna's and Vronsky's affair: separately or together, they either mourn the loss of or aspire again to the values and structure of marriage and family—those of Tolstoy's third period. Levin and Kitty are, of course, the major and most successful exponents of that kind of life. Though their concerns and interests are sharply distinguished from and extend beyond those of Anna and Vronsky, their legitimate aspirations toward personal and domestic well-being, property, and pleasure are nonetheless in conflict with Levin's nascent struggle toward the Christian ideals of Tolstoy's fourth period. For could one not say of Levin, as Tolstoy did of Nekhludov in *Resurrection*, that there are two natures in him? "One was spiritual, seeking only the kind of happiness which means happiness for everybody else as well, and the other was an animal nature, absorbed in self-gratification and seeking pleasure at the expense of the rest of the world" (JI 32:53). In this description of Nekhludov, Tolstoy has defined and enlarged the unripened conflict in Levin between his radiantly happy life with Kitty and his vision of a quasi-religious, even ascetic, way of life. In three stories of his late period—*The Kreutzer Sonata,* "The Devil," and "Father Sergius"—Tolstoy explored this tormenting conflict and attempted a final resolution.

Epilogue: Sexuality's Wasteland

> Being with him is like being on a plain where every-
> thing has been burned up by the sun, and where even the
> sun is burning itself out, threatening endless dark night.
>
> Gorky

Conceived within a single year, homogeneous in thought and style, three stories, *The Kreutzer Sonata,* "The Devil," and "Father Sergius," present Tolstoy's final fictional statement on the relations between men and women. *The Kreutzer Sonata* appeared first in 1889, followed a few months later by "The Devil." Although "Father Sergius" was not finished until 1897, it is clearly kin to the other two. It is important to think of these stories not only as individual works but, taken together, as an epilogue on sexuality, love, and marriage to Tolstoy's life-work.

Though Tolstoy had renounced all his belles lettres written before 1880, including *The Cossacks, Family Happiness, War and Peace,* and *Anna Karenina,* these three stories nevertheless took fictional form. It is understandable that the desire to renounce and suppress his artistic success would accompany the broader renunciation of his former style and philosophy of life and his adoption of a self-styled Christian pacifism. For tension and contradiction supply the texture of great fiction, and Tolstoy had not so much resolved his ambivalent views of woman, love, and sexuality, as allowed them to dissipate in his abandonment of the search for an ideal way of life which would include them. Yet Tolstoy could not extinguish the force of the artist within, and quite against his will and his new convictions *The Kreutzer Sonata,* "The Devil," and "Father Sergius" all took fictional form. The content and intent of these three stories, however, are in keeping with the didactic and polemical nature of Tolstoy's other prose of the period.[1]

To *The Kreutzer Sonata,* Tolstoy prefixed a stringent epigraph:

> But I say unto you, that whosoever looketh on a woman to lust after her hath committed adultery with her already in his heart. (Matt. 5.28)

The same epigraph precedes "The Devil"—with the addition of the two even more severe following verses, one of which recommends that

> if thy right hand offend thee, cut it off, and cast it from thee: for it is profitable for thee that one of thy members should perish, and not that thy whole body should be cast into hell. (Matt. 5.30)

In contrast to his earlier work, the two distinctive motifs of *The Kreutzer Sonata,* and equally of "The Devil" and "Father Sergius," are Tolstoy's explicit and exacerbated preoccupation with sex as central to the relations between men and women, and the barely concealed hysteria which provides the tone of the stories. They are the fulfillment of and the self-indulgent absorption in the dark content of *Family Happiness, War and Peace,* and, of course, *Anna Karenina.* Of the three pieces, *The Kreutzer Sonata* is the most developed and the most powerful. If one were not aware that the other two were written subsequently, one might consider them preliminary sketches for the first, so similar are the concerns and details. They are, however, more appropriately described as abortive attempts to remake the statements so compellingly rendered in *The Kreutzer Sonata.*

It is important to remember that Tolstoy wrote these stories when

1. Tolstoy's theory of art of this period is elaborated in his *What Is Art?* begun in 1896.

he himself was living a personal drama almost as complicated and debilitating as those of the stories themselves. He and his wife, at the respective ages of sixty-one and forty-five, quarreled bitterly about their manner of life, the education of their children, where they should live, indeed about the total moral structure of their life. He stubbornly professed that it must change, but never changed it, and his wife tried not only to carry on their former life but to convince her husband that it was necessary.

Ironically, Sofiya Andreyevna acted out in the mid-1890s her own pale version of *The Kreutzer Sonata* in her pathetic infatuation with Sergey Ivanovich Taneyev, concert pianist and family acquaintance. Though there was no sexual infidelity involved, the indiscretion of her desperate flirtation embarrassed and exasperated her family and friends, and disgusted her husband. The fact that he could be deeply upset about this "affair," however, indicates how closely they were still emotionally entangled with each other. The memoirs of their daughter, Tanya, present an unusually fair description of their life during this period:

> It is really destructive to live among people who hate one another while you wish well to both. They have reached such a stage of exacerbation that they have to weigh every word carefully before they speak, for fear of involuntarily hurting one another's feelings.

And a year later:

> I am all the more sorry for Mamma since, first, she does not believe in anything at all, either her own or Papa's ideas; second, she is the more lonely, because since she says and does so many things which are unreasonable, of course all the children are on Papa's side, and she feels her isolation terribly. And then she loves Papa more than he loves her, and is as delighted as a child if he addresses the least kind word to her.[2]

2. T. L. Sukhotin, *The Tolstoy Home: Diaries* (New York: Columbia University Press, 1951).

But this perhaps too-familiar story is noted here simply to invoke the chaotic context in which Tolstoy wrote these disturbed and disturbing tales.

The Kreutzer Sonata opens on a train, and for Tolstoy this generally means that normal modes of perception and reflection are distorted.[3] Later in the story, its anti-hero, Pozdnyshev himself, describes the change in his mood upon boarding a train eight hours before murdering his wife:

> But that tranquil mood, that ability to suppress my feelings ended with my drive. As soon as I entered the train, something entirely different began. That eight-hour journey in a railway carriage was something dreadful, which I shall never forget all my life. Whether it was that having taken my seat in the carriage, I vividly imagined myself as having already arrived, or that railway traveling has such an exhilarating effect on people, at any rate from the moment I sat down I could no longer control my imagination. [JI 27: 65–66]

In precisely this frame of mind, Pozdnyshev narrates his story against a background of confusion and semi-darkness. The train stops and starts, passengers come and go, candles sputter and die, conversations continue in darkness.

Aside from this murky setting, Pozdnyshev's personal appearance and habits contribute to the story's underground atmosphere. He is not actually introduced in the first scenes, but sits apart from his traveling companions, with his eyes glittering and strange sounds erupting from his throat, all the while smoking or drinking tea. He gives the impression of a chronic isolate, not belonging to this or any world. His clothes cross the limits of period and class: an old overcoat, "evidently from an expensive tailor," and underneath, a simple embroidered Russian shirt (JI 27: 7). There is nothing about

---

3. Anna Karenina's love affair, for example, has its beginning and ending in train stations. Like Pozdnyshev's, Anna's final condition is one of permanent transit.

him that marks his identity or suggests that he is a man of integrated character.

Carefully paced, like the piece that furnished its title, *The Kreutzer Sonata* unfolds its themes in precisely elaborated movements. Just as Pozdnyshev's identity is not fully revealed at the beginning neither is his story. Both are preceded and enhanced by a long overture. The tension of that overture is created by the motifs struck in the conversation among the passengers. The talk is concerned, in general, with men and women and their relations with each other. A lady and her companion, a lawyer, defend a "liberal" point of view, which is bitterly opposed by an old merchant whose attitude is more conventional. The discussion starts with the lawyer's remark that "then she plainly informed her husband that she was not able, and did not wish, to live with him." He goes on to say that "public opinion in Europe" was preoccupied with the question of divorce, and that cases of "that kind" were occurring more and more often in Russia (JI 27:9).

The old merchant takes a stern and disapproving view of this. To the lawyer who asks him if these things happened in the old days, he replies: "They used to happen even then, sir, but less often. The way things are now they can't help happening. People have got too educated" (JI 27:65–66). What follows is, in the form of argument, a distillation of the thinking and writing that Tolstoy had done about marital relations up to that point. The lady, in essence, defends a flexible approach to marriage. No woman, she contends, should be forced to marry someone she does not love; if she finds herself married to someone she does not love, or no longer loves, she should have the right to divorce, as should the husband in similar circumstances. The old merchant replies with stern platitudes: "Human beings have a law given them"; "the first thing that should be required of a woman is fear!" (of her husband, of course); the "female sex must be curbed in time or else all is lost!" When the narrator of the story reminds the old man that he was just boasting

about his own sexual exploits at a fair, the old man indignantly replies that that is "a special case" (JI 27: 9–12).

Certainly one feels at this moment in the story that the lady and
her friend are on firmer ground in the argument than the old man,
even though they have not won by any means. In this argument,
Tolstoy merely sets the scene and introduces the issues. But
Pozdnyshev, sitting apart from the others and now greatly agitated
by the discussion, will argue for him throughout the rest of the
story. The second section opens with his halting question: "What
kind of love . . . love . . . is it that sanctifies marriage?" (JI 27:
12). This question opens his long narration about his childhood and
debauched young manhood, his hypocrisy and deceit in his sexual
affairs, and his irresponsible relations with women in general. He
continues in great detail about the falsity of his marriage, his jealousy of his wife, and finally, his murder of her and his exile from
society. It is significant that *The Kreutzer Sonata* is, to a greater
degree than the other two stories, not only a personal confession but
an indictment of the culture as well.

At the opening of "The Devil," after giving up a promising career
in government service, Evgeny Irtenev is on his way to becoming a
successful gentleman-farmer. The estate that he has inherited from
his father, though burdened by debts, is slowly recovering. It is his
aim to re-create his grandfather's way of life, "when everything
was done on a grand scale, orderly and efficiently, and to everyone's
satisfaction" (JI 27: 482).

Irtenev's sexual biography is exactly the same as Posdnyshev's in
The Kreutzer Sonata, in spirit if not in actual detail. For his
"health" he had "arranged" his sex life to avoid moral or emotional
involvement with the women with whom he had relations. In the
country, when sexual desire begins to trouble him, he feels that it is
improper to arrange a liaison with one of his own peasants; but he
does it anyway, again "not out of lust but for health's sake" (JI 27:
483–84). Yet at this point his troubles begin, for although Irtenev

falls in love with his peasant mistress, Stepanida, he marries a "good" young woman, Liza Annenskaya, the daughter of a family in town.

On the surface, his marriage to Liza is a "happy" one: it is peaceful, satisfying, and provides a pleasant background and even inspiration for his work with the estate. But Irtenev's passion for Stepanida is constantly provoked by the sight of her bare legs as she washes his kitchen floor or of her red kerchief flashing as she dashes through the forest. Once he realizes that his feeling for her still disturbs him (and that she knows this), he is finally driven to drastic measures. He asks his uncle to chaperone him, he tries to have Stepanida's family moved out of the village, and, all else having failed, he escapes on a trip to the Crimea.

When Irtenev returns, his chances for success seem as good as at the beginning of the story: he is spiritually refreshed from his stay in the Crimea and fully believes that his feeling for Stepanida will no longer bother him. Indeed, at first sight of her, Irtenev "recognized who she was and was overjoyed to feel that he remained completely calm." But the next morning, "he saw once or twice the dark eyes and red kerchief of Stepanida, who was carrying hay. He glanced at her once or twice and felt something again; but he couldn't really define it. Only the next day when he again went to the threshing floor and stayed there unnecessarily for two hours, constantly caressing with his eyes the familiar, pretty figure of the young woman, did he feel himself lost, utterly, irretrievably lost" (JI 27:512). Directly after this scene, Irtenev shoots himself, and "no one could understand or explain the reason" (JI 27:514).

For "Father Sergius," Tolstoy could well have used again the same epigraph that he prefixed to *The Kreutzer Sonata* and to "The Devil." Stepan Kasatsky forsakes his name, his estate, his beautiful and loving fiancée, and a "brilliant career" (JI 31:5) like the one that awaited Evgeny Irtenev—all to become a monk and hermit in the Tambrino desert. The event that precipitates his dramatic conversion is thematically significant: he discovers that his fiancée, whom he loves deeply and who loves him in return, is not a virgin. Not only is she "impure," but she has been the mistress of the Tsar, whom Kasatsky loves and admires. One might expect that disclosure to soften the blow for the disappointed lover, but Kasatsky, his sense of humor and patriotism failing him equally, takes it as a double blow.

Just as Kasatsky had been a model dancer, soldier, and chess player, as Father Sergius he is a model monk. His only moral weakness is his excessive pride, which his spiritual adviser hoped would be subdued by isolation in the desert. Father Sergius's moral struggle centers around two things: "doubt, and the desires of the flesh" (JI 31 : 19). Temptation appears in the form of an enticing divorcée, Makovkina, who visits Father Sergius's cell and deliberately tries to seduce him. Her physical beauty and the rustling noises of her disrobing fill Sergius with the presentiment that "danger, ruin, was there, over him, around him, and that he could save himself only by not glancing at her for a single moment" (JI 31 : 25).

To prepare himself for the critical moment of encounter with the woman, Sergius follows Christ's advice (Matt. 5.30) and decides to cast off the symbolically offending organ, his finger. Just as Irtenev tried to distract himself from sexual desire by this same device, Sergius holds his finger in the candle flame; this failing, he chops the finger off with an ax. The terrible pain, the flow of blood, and the relief of moral tension enable him actually to talk with the woman. Father Sergius's desperate strategy is so successful that he, in effect, converts her to a religious life: "A year later she was invested in a small nunnery and lived a strict life in the monastery" (JI 31 : 26).

Throughout the seven or eight years following this episode with Makovkina, and in part because of it, Father Sergius acquires fame as a holy man and even as a miracle-worker. But as his reputation for holiness increases, the actual conditions of his life become less and less ascetic; he is a prime drawing-card for the Church and is treated as such. He eats well, if not luxuriously; he has a servant; and his cell is remodeled for capacity crowds. Yet he does not resist this treatment, and even when he does it is simply pretense; his vanity still pursues him.

Father Sergius's final "fall," like Pozdnyshev's and Irtenev's, is an erotic lapse caused by the devil in the guise of a woman, this time the feeble-minded but voluptuous daughter of a merchant who wants Sergius to cure her. When he first learns about her, he is "pleased to learn that the merchant's daughter was twenty-two years old, and he was anxious to know if she was pretty. Furthermore, in inquiring about her weakened condition, he had hoped to find out whether or not she was endowed with feminine charm" (JI 31 : 35). Already excited in his imagination by the girl, he readily succumbs to her when in his cell she embraces him and draws him to his "solitary couch" (JI 31 : 36). After his seduction, Father Sergius runs away in fear and confusion and is told in a dream to go to Pashenka Mikhailovna, an old acquaintance, to discover his fate. Her kindness and humility show him the true way, he becomes a simple pilgrim, is eventually arrested, and is sent to Siberia, where he "teaches little children and attends the sick" (JI 31 : 46).

In each of these three sister works, the main male characters are or were personally and socially brilliant aristocrats, whose lives and careers are ruined by events that center around a woman. Pozdnyshev murders his wife because of his rage at her response to another man. Stepan Kasatsky (Father Sergius) has three painful and destructive crises with women: the disclosure of his fiancée's love affair with the Tsar, his temptation by the divorcée, and his seduction by a suppliant girl. Evgeny Irtenev has an uncontrollable passion for his serf, Stepanida, which drives him to suicide.

And it is not merely that these women act as the incidental catalysts of disaster; they are endowed with demonic powers. A decade after *The Kreutzer Sonata,* Tolstoy claimed in his *Journal* that "woman . . . is the tool of the devil. She is usually stupid, but the devil lends her his brain when she works for him. Thanks to this, she has accomplished miracles of intellect, perspective, and constancy—in order to do something vile. . . . But when there is no need for something vile, she cannot understand the simplest thing . . . and has no self-control . . . (JI 53: 208). In *The Kreutzer Sonata* Pozdnyshev asserts that "a woman is happy and attains all she can desire when she has bewitched a man. Therefore the chief aim of a woman is to bewitch him" (JI 27: 38). Father Sergius exclaims to his seductress, "You are a devil" (JI 31: 36). Before, when the beautiful divorcée, Makovkina, came to his hermit cell to seduce him, he had asked, "Can it be true then as I read in the lives of the saints that the devil takes the form of a woman?" (JI 31: 20). Of course, the title of "The Devil" speaks for itself, but Evgeny's accusation of Stepanida makes the association clear: "She is a devil anyway. Just that, a devil. Hasn't she subjugated me against my will?" (JI 27: 513).

Of the three stories, however, *The Kreutzer Sonata* most clearly reveals in Pozdnyshev's image of his wife the source of this identification: the temptation of woman's sexuality. It is important to note that Pozdnyshev does not refer to his wife by name. She is neither personalized nor distinguished from any other woman. Anonymously and archetypally, she is Sexual Woman. Underneath the trappings of dress, manner, and feminine charm, there lies, in her husband's view, a malicious plan to keep him, and all men, from worthwhile and dignifying pursuits. In the full bloom of her maturity, with her children no longer an effective curb to her energies, and with the fear of further pregnancies removed, she is described by her husband as a "fresh, well fed harness horse, whose bridle has been removed" (JI 27: 47). (Pozdnyshev's image calls to mind the elaborate parallel between Anna and Vronsky's mare.) *The Kreutzer Sonata*'s most serious indictment of rampant sexuality is that it alone, as the strongest and most violent of the passions, has kept humanity from reaching its goal of "goodness, righteousness, and love" (JI 27: 30).

Especially in *The Kreutzer Sonata,* Tolstoy once again dismisses the reality of romantic love, or poetic love, or falling in love. In *Family Happiness,* Sergey Mikhailych and Masha fell in love, and their initial feeling for each other corresponded to the traditional view of "poetic" or romantic love. For both the lovers, however, the illusion that attended this phase in their lives, the illusion that each partner was precisely what the other wanted and would never change, was cruelly betrayed. In *The Kreutzer Sonata* there is no longer any such illusion; at least, Pozdnyshev in retrospect analyzes the illusion as something far different from romantic love. When courting his future wife, it had seemed to him on occasion that "she understood all that I felt and thought, and that what I felt and thought was very lofty. In reality it was only that her dress and her curls were particularly becoming to her and that after a day spent near her I wanted to be still closer." And further along: "The most exalted poetic love, as we call it, depends not on moral qualities but on physical nearness and on the coiffure, and the color and cut of the dress" (JI 27: 21, 22).

In addition to reducing the act of falling in love to pure sexual attraction, Tolstoy is led from this hypothesis to suggest that all aspects of love—warmth of communication, friendship, joy in intimacy—are mere reflections or distortions of sexuality. Pozdnyshev, for example, found it impossible for himself and his wife to engage in simple conversation as an expression of the "spiritual communion" that should accompany romantic love: "Well, if love is spiritual, spiritual communion, then that spiritual communion should find expression in words, in conversations, in discourse. There was nothing of the kind. It used to be dreadfully difficult to talk when we were left alone. . . . There was nothing to talk about" (JI 27: 27).

Tolstoy moreover denied the possibility of communication on a deeper level, that is, the commitment and exchange that follows the recognition of a partner whose ideals meet and enhance one's own. To the woman on the train who defended this possibility, Pozdny-shev angrily, and straight to the point, retorted: "Spiritual affinity! Identity of ideals! . . . But in that case why go to bed together? (Excuse my vulgarity!)" (JI 27: 14).

It may seem contradictory that even in these late stories, Tolstoy could still envision love as *agape* (if not *eros*); that is, that he could still occasionally entertain the possibility of married love built on spiritual communication and on deep reverential friendship. Such is, perhaps, the meaning of the relation of Evgeny Irtenev's wife, Liza, to her husband: emotionally warm but sexually cool. The portrait of Liza herself is almost unbelievably angelic. She is close to Tolstoy's ideal woman (along with her predecessors, Princess Marya of *War and Peace* and Pashenka of "Father Sergius"). Physically, she is presentable but not sexually attractive. Her eyes, like Princess Marya's, are her best feature: they are bright, tender, trustful, in contrast to the "black, sparkling" eyes of her rival, the serf Stepanida (JI 27: 487). Liza's eyes appeal and confide, while Stepanida's provoke and invite. Emotionally, Liza is sentimental, without passion; her infatuations with men before her marriage to Evgeny develop into tender, loving concern and pride when directed exclusively toward her husband. Her emotional make-up is primarily devoted and maternal, and her goal in her relations with her husband, indeed, of her life, is to make for him the best of all possible lives: "Liza had decided that of all the people in the world there was only her Evgeny Irtenev, a higher type, wiser, purer, nobler than all the others; and it therefore was the responsibility of everyone to serve him and to make life pleasant for him" (JI 27: 494). Liza is endowed with that "spiritual communion" which Pozdnyshev found lacking between himself and his wife. In her relations with Evgeny, "she sensed every one of his moods, every shade of feeling, often, he thought, more clearly than he did himself. . . . Moreover, she understood his thoughts as well as his feelings" (JI 27: 494). One might assume from this that Liza's and Evgeny's marriage should proceed tranquilly and tenderly, for Evgeny truly loves his wife as a warm and loyal friend. And that is precisely the problem; their close communication is warped by Evgeny's displaced sexual passion for Stepanida. This reveals Tolstoy's belief that these two forms of love and expression can never flow toward the same person. It is this tragic and unbearable division that dooms Evgeny.

Behind Tolstoy's idea of this apparently inevitable division, one may discern his view of sexuality and the sexual act itself. The sexual biography of each of the three men in these stories, particularly that of Pozdnyshev and Evgeny, reflects Tolstoy's view in some detail. The following passages are both typical and crucial: Evgeny, for instance,

> had spent his youth as do all young healthy bachelors; that is, he had had relationships with various kinds of women. He was not a debauchee, but neither was he . . . a monk! He indulged in this . . . only as far as it was necessary for his physical health and peace of mind. This began when he was sixteen, and had continued successfully, in the sense that he had not drowned himself in orgies, had never fallen in love, and had never caught any disease. As a result this phase of his life had been securely settled and had given him no trouble. [JI 27: 483]

And Pozdnyshev says about his young manhood:

> I was not a seducer, had no unnatural tastes, did not make that the main purpose of my life as many of my associates did, but I practiced debauchery in a steady, decent way for my health's sake. I avoided women who might tie my hands by having a child or by attachment for me. There may have been children and attachments, however, but I acted as if there were not. And this I considered not only moral, I was even proud of it. [JI 27: 16]

The description of Kasatsky's youth adds a new dimension: the double standard in its classic form, which introduces, in addition to premarital sexual partners, the woman who was *not* a part of the "debauched" life, the woman one could marry:

Kasatsky belonged to those people of the forties who no longer exist, who, while consciously indulging in and inwardly not condemning unchaste sexual relations, demanded an ideal, heavenly chastity in a wife, recognized this heavenly chastity in every young girl of their own circles, and treated them accordingly. There was much that was false in this attitude, and it was harmful in the profligacy which it permitted men; but in respect to women, this viewpoint, which differs so sharply from that of today's youth, who see their potential mate in every young girl . . . did serve a purpose. Aware of this attitude, young girls tried more or less to be goddesses. [JI 31:9]

Pozdnyshev, too, says that he wallowed in a mire of debauchery and at the same time was looking for a girl chaste enough "to be worthy of [him]" (JI 27:20).

The nineteenth-century version of the double standard has always plagued men and women; but Tolstoy articulated its most painful consequences. Pozdnyshev (speaking for Tolstoy) confesses that, for himself, "dissoluteness does not lie in anything physical—no kind of physical misconduct is debauchery; real debauchery lies precisely in freeing oneself from moral relations with a woman with whom you have physical intimacy" (JI 27:17). In Tolstoy's view, *this* constituted the real double standard, and the only significant one. It was not only a double standard applied in relation to other persons, but was the mark of an interior division between act, feeling, and moral responsibility.

This tragic split is portrayed in the relationship of Evgeny Irtenev and Stepanida. Irtenev deliberately arranges a meeting with one of his own serfs (his forefathers' principles to the contrary) and uses her purely as a safety valve to release the pressure of his drive, "for

his health's sake."[4] The arrangements are made in the way that
Irtenev might buy a new team of horses. Danila, the peasant pro-
curer, asks if Evgeny has any special requirements. He replies that
it doesn't matter, though "of course, she should be healthy and not
ugly!" Danila, after some thought, suggests that Stepanida is not
only "clean," but a "good lover" (JI 27: 484–85). But when the possibility of the fusion of erotic pleasure and emotional or moral involvement is suggested, Evgeny becomes confused and defensive:

> "No, no . . . that's not at all what I need. On the contrary." (What
> could be on the contrary?) "I need, on the contrary . . . just let
> her be healthy, no fuss and bother—a soldier's wife or the like."
> [JI 27: 485]

Stepanida proves to be very satisfactory and after their first meeting,
Irtenev, now serene, once again turns freely to his business. "Only
at first was there any shame, but it passed" (JI 27: 485).

An apparently unrelated scene between Evgeny and his mother
follows directly after this meeting with Stepanida. They discuss one
of his father's debts: twelve thousand rubles owed the widow
Esipova, his grandfather's ward. His mother explains to Evgeny
that there is no real debt, but that his father regarded it as one.
Evgeny assures her that he understands it in the same way and that
he "must" pay her. His mother feels "consoled and proud of her
son's decision" because he has lived up to what she, his father, and
he himself considered a moral obligation (JI 27: 486). He feels a
sense of responsibility to this widow whom he has never seen and
whose demands, his mother hints, are probably parasitical.

This is a relatively trivial matter and, indeed, seems completely
irrelevant to the main thread of the story. But it does serve as a comment on the immediately preceding episode, which describes the relations between Irtenev and Stepanida. More than a comment; it is

4. The autobiographical parallel is, of course, Tolstoy's affair with Aksinya
Bazykin. See chap. 4, note 9.

an indictment of the false morality which would allow a man to enter into intimate relations with one of his serfs with total moral detachment, and which would, on the other hand, demand that he fulfill a "moral" obligation to a woman of his own class whom he has never encountered and whose rights he is not even sure of.

As we have seen, this divided ethic is also expressed in Evgeny's dream of marriage. Like Pozdnyshev and Kasatsky, he hoped eventually to marry a woman very different from the one whom he was meeting in the woods. And it would be revolting to him, he feels, to marry for money; he wanted to marry "honestly, for love" (JI 27: 487). On the other hand, overcoming his initial reluctance, he converts the master/serf arrangement into sexual therapy. But much to his surprise, he finds that his relations with Stepanida not only continue but take on a personal character: "He liked her, and he thought that he needed such a liaison and that there was nothing wrong in it. But deep in his soul was a more severe judge that disapproved and hoped this was the last time, or if he did not really hope for this, at least he did not want to participate directly in fixing another meeting" (JI 27: 488).

Why such a tragic sexual schizophrenia? The later Tolstoy, as we know, regarded sexual intercourse, even between married partners, as disgusting and absurd, a shameful, "animal" act that separated the partners spiritually and emotionally. But that did not eliminate the basic problem of sexuality, the recognition of oneself and others as sexual creatures, fully available to each other. This might be called the "no barriers" theme in Tolstoy's thought, for he uses the phrase again and again to denote such recognition. This phrase indicates the mutual sudden awareness of attraction between many couples in Tolstoy's works: Pierre and Ellen, Natasha and Anatole, Anna and Vronsky, and so on. In short, throughout Tolstoy's literary work, he defines sexual attraction with a phrase connoting the consciousness of a naked confrontation between the two persons and of an uncontrolled force drawing them together.

After his wife's concert with his imagined rival, for example, Pozdnyshev feels that it was "evident already then, that there was . . . no barrier between them" (JI 27:64). In "Father Sergius," the event is described without the specific phrase; Makovkina triumphantly realizes that when she knocked at Father Sergius's door "he put his face to the window and saw me and understood and recognized me, it was glowing and imprinted in his eyes. He loved and desired me. Yes, desired" (JI 31:23–24).

Of course this naked confrontation is not always matched by a frank admission of the basically erotic content of sex. The men of these stories invent verbal subterfuges, like the "safety valve" metaphor that occurs so often in Tolstoy, or better yet, they repeat the maxim that sex is necessary for the sake of one's health. In the notion that sex is necessary to the health, the mechanical idea of sex as a "safety valve" is simply rendered more explicit and concrete. Expressing these attitudes, Tolstoy was not merely reflecting his society: he was stating previous or present personal convictions. In *The Second Supplement to The Kreutzer Sonata,* he wrote: "The sexual instinct seems to me like the pressure of steam, which would cause a locomotive to explode if the pressure did not open the safety valve. The valve opens only under great pressure; otherwise it is always kept closed, and carefully closed, and it must be our conscious aim to keep it tightly closed and held down moreover by a weighted layer . . . so that it cannot open."[5]

Both theories depersonalize man, woman, and act: first, although at this late stage Tolstoy emphasized keeping the valve closed as much as possible, in the "safety valve" theory the use of the mechanical metaphor reduces the sexual act to an annoying but necessary device which keeps the machine running smoothly. Sex "for the health" implies both that the body is, in some sense, sick, and that the therapy is simply a matter of taking the appropriate treatment. Tolstoy's imagery evokes the dangers of a high-pressure steam

5. Tolstoy, *Church and State,* p. 166.

boiler and suggests the regular maintenance of delicate plumbing. To ward off these perils, to service the machinery—this is woman's sexual function. Both of these dehumanizing attitudes have at their core the idea of selfish use: a woman is used by a man to keep him functioning properly. Finally, however, the sexual bond is human, not mechanical. Yet in their rationalizations Tolstoy's characters are reluctant to admit that they feel such humanity. When Evgeny, for example, as pointed out before, seeks a woman for his "health," Danila suggests a clean healthy woman, and goes on to describe her sexual appeal. But Evgeny cuts him off because it reminds him of the purely erotic motives, the real nature of his request: " 'No, no . . . that's not all what I need. On the contrary.' (What could be the contrary?)" (JI 27: 485). But beyond eroticism loomed the possibility of an involvement, an emotional commitment which would inevitably fail.

In his earlier fiction, the familiar Tolstoyan solution to this dilemma was marriage, chiefly for two reasons: marriage could organize and focus the sex drive, and it could provide further justification for sex and compensation for the failure of romantic love in the creation of a family. If one takes *The Kreutzer Sonata* at face value, however, marriage as a solution to man's sexual problems is no longer possible. In the first place, love itself, and the desire to be together with one's beloved for a lifetime, are explained away as the result of an explosive pressure without a safety valve: "Try and close the safety valve . . ." Pozdnshev warns, "and at once a stimulus arises which, passing through the prism of our artificial life, expresses itself in utter infatuation, sometimes even platonic." And he continues, further on, "Had the safety valve been open . . . I should not have fallen in love" (JI 27: 23–24).

On this foundation, marriage would have little chance for mere survival. Pozdnyshev grudgingly admits that there are a few "true" marriages, providing a good Tolstoyan definition of an ideal marriage: "something mysterious, a sacrament binding [the partners] in the sight of God" (JI 27: 14–15). This kind of marriage, though, is very rare; according to Pozdnyshev "ninety-nine percent of married people live in a similar hell" to the one that he experienced in his own marriage (JI 27: 45). That is, marriage is deception, a thin veil of convention, screening its real object, copulation. Such a marriage knows neither friendship nor fidelity, only an ever-increasing hatred, relieved by periods of sexual activity which, in turn, breeds further hatred. Far from softening its brutal outlines, the children of such a marriage are "not a joy but a torment" (JI 27: 43). In the midst of the tensions between husband and wife, they become the object of discord and simultaneously the weapons of strife. In short, where there is sex, there can be neither love, nor marital happiness, nor the joy of family.

In *The Kreutzer Sonata* Tolstoy refers to the *Domostroy*, a sixteenth-century marriage and domestic manual. Its straightforward, no-nonsense manner of dealing with marriage is apparently prompted by a romantic notion of the past. The old man on the train, for example, who defends his old-fashioned views of marriage (women should fear their husbands, matchmaking is a sensible way to get a hard job done) is referred to by his female opponent as a "living Domostroy" (JI 27: 12). Pozdnyshev refers to the *Domostroy* in another context: "You must remember that if one married according to the injunctions of the *Domostroy*, as that old fellow was saying, then the feather-beds, the trousseau, and the bedstead are all merely details appropriate to the sacrament" (JI 27: 27). For his contemporaries, however, these objects are the medium of exchange in the sale of an innocent girl to a profligate. One should think of Tolstoy's nostalgic view of the *Domostroy* in this case as another example of his general wish during this period to return to a past of Arcadian simplicity and virtue, to get back to the roots, to re-create the beginnings of things. He no longer, however, actually believes in the real possibility of such a way of life. These abandoned hopes float like dream-fragments around his much more persuasive portrait of marriage as disillusion and deception.

Indeed, so powerful was the terror of sexuality and its derivative bonds in marriage that during his later period Tolstoy could readily conceive only of extreme or violent means of breaking the stalemate which they produced. Of Pozdnyshev, Irtenev, or Father Sergius, one could say as Tolstoy did of Hans Christian Andersen that "he was a confirmed rake and wanderer . . . but that only strengthens my conviction that he was a lonely man." [6] For each of these characters is driven to isolate himself from those he loves and even from the rest of mankind: driven to the isolation of exile following the murder of his wife, driven to the ultimate isolation of death by suicide, or driven to the isolation of an ascetic religious commitment. In his youth and manhood, Tolstoy himself considered suicide; this impulse was closely linked to a sense of meaninglessness in his life, to which the problem of sexuality had contributed.[7] And he contemplated religious asceticism as a possible escape from the torment of marriage. On one occasion (to be sure, eighteen years after writing *The Kreutzer Sonata*) he said to his friend and biographer N. N. Gusev: "I ought to have gone into a monastery. And I would have, if I hadn't had a wife."[8]

Of course, religious asceticism is the particular form of escape chosen by Stepan Kasatsky, who becomes Father Sergius. He chooses an ascetic life, as noted before, as a result of discovering that his fiancée is not a virgin, and that, moreover, she was mistress of the Tsar. Kasatsky's conversion to the religious life is scarcely convincing, however, since it appears to be only another manifestation of pride, based ultimately on his desire for superiority and on an insatiable will to perfection. Like Masha's attempt to lead a pious life in *Family Happiness,* Sergius's religious commitment is

6. Gorkij, *Lev Tolstoj,* p. 256.
7. Discussed in his *Confession.*
8. To N. N. Gusev, 1907.

always in danger of increasing his concern for himself rather than his concern for God, for mankind, or for a purified way of life.

Although Father Sergius had originally become a hermit because he had been disillusioned with a woman who did not measure up to an ideal of perfect purity, he also suffers from the discrepancy within himself between formal intent and the winds of passion. Understandably, as a monk he still fears close personal contact with a real (that is, imperfect) woman, for he cannot trust his impulses and his self-control. With Makovkina, the contact is immediately sexual in tone, and Sergius's actions and words, surely designed to bolster his wavering self-control, have not only the effect which he desired for himself but, ironically, the additional consequence of converting Makovkina to a nun's life. Thus he secured safety for himself, and protected his own isolation, by persuading the dangerous and tempting Makovkina to take on his own austere commitment. Thereafter, surrounded by adoring crowds who seek his miraculous powers, Sergius remains utterly alone, like the Dostoevskyan saints who love mankind but cannot abide their neighbor.

But his position is false and finally untenable. The incident with the half-witted girl, his second temptation, reads, of course, like a caricature of the first. For one thing, with the half-wit, there could be an impersonal sexual act, but no serious personal exchange. In addition, finding his general situation morally and emotionally intolerable, he could extricate himself from it by permitting his own seduction. The outcome was to be, in any case, a manageable life of limited risks and limited options without temptations, and without the implicit reproach of adoring multitudes. In his Siberian exile, he tends vegetables, children, and the sick, none of these a challenge to his sexuality or his humanity.

Secular celibacy is an equally possible solution for the male, as Pozdnyshev implies at the end of *The Kreutzer Sonata*. The reader is surprised to learn that immediately after stabbing his wife Pozdnyshev suddenly becomes aware of her as a human being and of the atrocity of his act. But from this belated insight, he concludes not that he should have refrained from murder, but that he should never have married! That is, only celibacy, not an agreement worked out within the marriage, could have prevented murder.

While "Father Sergius" is a curiously undigested piece, its theme of isolation receives a more significant and careful treatment in *The Kreutzer Sonata*. As previously described, Pozdnyshev appears as a loner, his albatross his only companion, the train his only home, even his natural habitat. The fact that we do not know its destination, that its few stopping places are, of course, only temporary, and that its atmosphere makes civilized communication practically impossible, are all appropriate to his previous and present life. Indeed, on a deeper level, the train is an engine of meaningless transit, from which, so long as it is in motion, one cannot escape; it is the allegory of a life over which one has no conscious control.

Dostoevsky's preoccupation with two forms of absolute violence, murder and suicide, is well known. On the other hand, because these themes are not prominent in Tolstoy's novels, he is usually assumed to have been free of the preoccupation with personal and metaphysical violence. Yet clearly in these three late stories, murder and suicide are thematically central. Pozdnyshev's final isolation, resulting from the murder of his wife, fulfills the story which he feels compelled to tell. It would, however, be a mistake to conclude that Tolstoy presents this isolation as, in any simple sense, the punishment for Pozdnyshev's crime. In fact, like the heroes of the other two stories, Pozdnyshev himself has manipulated the events leading to his isolation. On the simplest level within all three stories, the idea or act of violence has essentially the same meaning, for all three men—Pozdnyshev, Sergius, Irtenev—have manipulated their lives to a point where violence is a natural and immediate possibility. They all contemplate both murder and suicide, and two of them commit, in addition, the symbolic suicide of self-mutilation.

As each contemplates or commits the murder, the actual or proposed victim is a woman whose femininity and sexuality have
provoked the man to the conclusion that life is unbearable.
  But suicide and murder are not, in these stories, the apocalyptic
objective of events. Rather, the act of killing is instrumental. Indeed, murder and suicide share indistinguishably the same purpose.
Tolstoy presents both acts, killing onself or killing another, as the
means of solving an otherwise inescapable problem, to which an
agony of paralysis is the only alternative. Here, violence is the
means of breaking past a stalemate, or a way of bringing an intolerable series of events, an intolerable situation, to a close. Thus,
like the sex in these stories, violence is finally impersonal, without
real reference to the individuality of its object. In short, murder or
suicide is a mode of manipulating the self, others, and events, so
that in each case, the outcome leaves the agent free of self, others,
and events: totally isolated.
  Pozdnyshev clearly recognizes his own active agency in creating
the events that simultaneously cause his downfall and justify it. He
recalls, for instance, that

> a strange and fatal force led me not to repulse him [Trukhachev-
> sky], not to keep him away, but on the contrary to invite him to
> the house . . . as if almost compulsively, I began talking about his
> playing. [JI 27: 53]

> I invited him to come some evening and bring his violin to play
> with my wife. She glanced at me with surprise, flushed, and as if
> frightened began to decline, saying that she did not play well
> enough. This refusal irritated me further and I insisted even more
> on his coming. [JI 27: 54]

More conclusive, and more final, is the following confession:

> If he had not appeared, there would have been someone else. If the
> occasion had not been jealousy, it would have been something else.

I maintain that all husbands who live as I did must either live
dissolutely, separately, or kill themselves or their wives as I have
done. [JI 27: 50]

Pozdnyshev's admission completely separates the act of murder
from the events that preceded and provoked it, since the murder has
no cause apart from his own need to escape his wife's temptation
and to release him from an impossible commitment. Hence, the
murder cannot be entirely and exclusively identified with the sexual
act, but it is analogous to it as another product of the gulf between
act, feeling, and responsibility.[9]

In Tolstoy's fiction from *Family Happiness* to *Anna Karenina,*
women are primarily, and in more concrete ways than men, responsible for the failures of love and marriage. In this respect, the
three late stories mark a striking departure. For in them Tolstoy
indicts both woman and man; the man, in love or marriage, is no
longer merely passive or unaware, essentially a victim, but personally responsible and even manipulative. Though these three
characters are, properly speaking, anti-heroes, each experiences a
moment of transformative self-awareness. Only for Father Sergius,
however, does this self-recognition lead to a final redemption. All
three men achieve self-awareness through discovery of the tragic
discrepancy between what they are and what they thought or
wanted themselves to be. This, in turn, leads each to an awakening,
a conversion to a different way of life, thought, and action, and, in
the case of Irtenev, to the end of life itself. The exiled Sergius is a
partial exception, for by radically limiting both his hopes and his
field of action, he overcomes the discrepancy between actuality and
aspiration.

To have admitted and expressed man's share in the failure of love

9. The sexual dimension of murder is discussed by J. Bayley in *Tolstoy and
the Novel* (London: Chatto and Windus, 1966).

and marriage was a great change for Tolstoy. Ironically, he writes like a radical feminist when, in *The Second Supplement to The Kreutzer Sonata,* he argues that

> the man who has hitherto led a debauched life passes on moral corruption to the woman, infects her with his own sensuality, and taxes her with the unbearable burden of being at one and the same time mistress, mother, and human being; and she develops, too, into an excellent mistress, a tortured mother, and a suffering, nervous, and hysterical human being. And the man loves her as his mistress, ignores her as a mother, and hates her for her nervousness and hysteria which he himself has caused. It seems to me that this is the source of all the sufferings that arise in every family.[10]

This recognition does not, however, soften Tolstoy's views of women. That is, he finds himself and all men guilty in their premarital and family relations, and for the first time he describes this guilt. Nonetheless, within this new view, he sees women as willing accomplices, as accessories before, during, and after the fact. Though men are *more* responsible for failure than in his earlier writings, women are no less responsible, and only the men are given the opportunity and the sensitivity to change or grow.

Taken together, these three stories constituted Tolstoy's final negation of the most fundamental human institutions, commitments, and values. Implicitly and explicitly in these tales, he denied either the practical possibility or the value of chastity, love, marriage, intimacy, sexuality, and fidelity. Understandably, the public reacted strongly to the black pessimism of *The Kreutzer Sonata,* and Tolstoy was asked to explain and interpret the tale. Though he had ignored or refused requests to comment formally on earlier works, his response to this furor was an explanatory "Epilogue," which he wrote in 1890.

10. Tolstoy, *Church and State,* p. 165.

Tolstoy designed the Epilogue to contain "the essence of what [he] had intended to convey." [11] In the first place, he writes, he wanted to oppose the notion that sex is necessary to health, and correspondingly to deny that social arrangements based on this premise are justified. Second, he argues that marital infidelity occurs because people mistakenly believe that sexual love is romantic and elevating, whereas it is in fact brutish and degrading. He goes so far as to say that "the violation of a promise of fidelity, given in marriage, should be punished by public opinion certainly in no lesser degree than are punished the violations of debts and business frauds." [12] This harsh mandate for human judgment is far from the cooler tone of *Romans* 12.19, which appeared as the epigraph to *Anna Karenina*. Earlier, as we have seen, he had been content to leave judgment of such sins to God; or, more accurately, to the logic and finality of the events themselves.

As his third point, Tolstoy warns against the bad effects of birth control. His admonitions draw on his contempt for medical practice; he asserts that sexual relations make pregnant or nursing women hysterical; and he regards contraception as equivalent to murder. The fourth and fifth points are not really distinct either from each other or from the second: he says that children are educated, by clothes, sweets, excesses of food and drink, music, novels, poems, and so forth, to a life of sensuality; and that "the best part of young people's lives is passed, by men, in discovering love-affairs or marriage, and by women and girls, in alluring and draw-

11. V. Šklovskij, in his biography *Lev Tolstoj* (Moscow: Molodaja Gvardija, 1963), p. 644, suggests that it was difficult for Tolstoy to write this Epilogue—as if he had to force himself, driving home point after point. Perhaps it is more satisfactory to assume that in breaking his customary silence about the "meaning" of his fiction, Tolstoy was revealing the compelling need to express his ideas. His need to write an Epilogue suggests that, in this case, the act of writing led Tolstoy to inadequate catharsis and failed to free him from his preoccupation with sexuality.

12. JI 27: 80. JI 27 contains the Epilogue with its interesting variants.

ing men into love-affairs or marriage" (JI 27:82). He repeats his
belief that sexual love is not a worthy activity of human beings
(men) but, quite to the contrary, keeps them from their only proper
pursuit: to serve humanity, country, science, art, or God.

Needless to say, *The Kreutzer Sonata,* considered together with
the other two stories, carries a much larger meaning than the
strident and erratically argued Epilogue. In fact, the three stories,
viewed together, may be regarded as offering a spectrum of final
statements on the problem posed by women, sexuality, and moral
schizophrenia. It is, however, both striking and characteristic that
by the late 1880s Tolstoy could present his solutions only as utterly
impracticable or productive of misery.

Basic to the shared content of the three stories is Tolstoy's assurance that women, and the sexuality that women represent, project, and provoke, are the source of man's downfall. Because of
them, careers are destroyed, character is corrupted, sexual desire
flares out of control. In *War and Peace* and *Anna Karenina* Tolstoy
was still willing to represent marriage as an effective and acceptable
way to organize sex for the purpose of bearing children. In two of
these three stories, however, though the marriages could have taken
such a form, Tolstoy's characters dismiss this possibility without
serious consideration. In each of the three stories, when the main
character faces a dilemma that is mainly sexual in nature, he feels
a profound fear, distrust, or contempt of sexuality, or of intimacy
of any kind. And in all three, as a direct consequence of, and indeed in direct response to, the sexual dilemma of the male tempted
by the female, alienation and violence follow relentlessly.

Natasha and Pierre and Kitty and Levin had escaped this fate;
Anna and Vronsky had succumbed to it. Yet there was adequate
warning of this nihilism even as early as *Family Happiness,* where
the possibility of happiness is concrete at the beginning, but where
the deterioration of romantic illusion and the isolation of mates is
inexorable. In *The Kreutzer Sonata* and its satellites, the possibility

of alternatives or adjustment to this process appears as delusion or hallucination. But *The Kreutzer Sonata* penetrates beyond a tragic view of experience: like Tolstoy's own *Confession,* its orgiastic tone and its insistent self-contempt invite us to celebrate, with the penitents, their capacity for evil and their pride of guilt. In these three stories, the consistent single message is the inevitable failure of human relationships and the inescapable recognition of human alienation. In this world, like Pashenka and Father Sergius, who come together only for aid and comfort, men and women no longer live and act in concert, but in isolation.

Other great writers have substituted one vision of life for another, or have dedicated themselves to an ideal which the force of ambivalence may have destroyed. But few have equaled that relentless testing of moral sensibility and human capacity, that indefatigable urge to break beyond limitations that characterized Tolstoy's life and fiction. In his own typically distilled yet sweeping formulation, "life is the expansion of limits" (JI 54:29). Even late in Tolstoy's life when that expansion absorbed limits and became grotesque, one feels with Gorky that "the disagreeable or hostile feelings which he aroused would assume forms that were not oppressive but seemed to explode within one's soul, expanding it, giving it greater capacity." Yet his power was tragically flawed by his consistently limited and distorted view of the nature of sex, of women, and, therefore, of the men who were his chief concern. So that, by the end of his life, the dream of the young Tolstoy—of a warm family life in the country, of a productive and benevolent estate, of friendships, of literary success, of the pursuit of culture—had vanished entirely. For this ideal, the spent but still aspiring old man finally substituted his heterodox-Christian vision of an emotionally and erotically anaesthetic world.

Selected Bibliography

Aldanov, M. A. *Zagadka Tolstogo*. Berlin: I. P. Ladyžnikov, 1923.

Arnold, Matthew. *Essays in Criticism*. London: Macmillan, 1894.

Asquith, Cynthia. *Married to Tolstoy*. London: Hutchinson, 1960.

Bayley, John. *Tolstoy and the Novel*. London: Chatto and Windus, 1966.

Birjukov, P. *Lev Nikolaevič Tolstoj,* vols. I–IV. Moscow: Posrednik, 1911–23.

Blackmur, R. P. "'*Anna Karenina*': The Dialectic of Incarnation," *Kenyon Review* XII (1950), 433–56.

Blumberg, E. J. "Tolstoy and the English Novel: A Note on *Middlemarch* and *Anna Karenina,*" *Slavic Review* 3 (Sept., 1971), 561–69.

———. "The Ideal Woman in Tolstoy," M.A. thesis, New York: Columbia University, 1968.

Christian, R. F. *Tolstoy's 'War and Peace.'* Oxford: Clarendon Press, 1962.

Dunham, V. S. "The Strong Woman Motif," in *The Transformation of Russian Society,* ed. Cyril Black. Cambridge, Mass.: Harvard University Press, 1960.

Ejxenbaum, B. M. *Skvoz' literaturu*. Leningrad: Academia, 1924.

———. *Lev Tolstoj,* 3 vols. Leningrad: Priboj, 1928, 1931; Sovetskij pisatel', 1960.

Ermilov, V. *Tolstoj—xudožnik i roman 'Vojna i mir.'* Moscow: GIXL, 1961.

Gifford, Henry. "Anna, Lawrence and 'The Law,'" *Critical Quarterly* I (1959), 203–6.

———. "Further Notes on 'Anna Karenina,'" *Critical Quarterly* II (1960), 158–60.

Gol'denvejzer, A. B. *Vblizi Tolstogo*. Moscow: GIXL, 1959.

Gor'kij, M. *Lev Tolstoj. Sobranie sočinenija*. Moscow: 1951.

Greenwood, E. B. "The Unity of 'Anna Karenina,'" *Landfall* XV (1961), 124–34.

Gusev, N. N. *Letopis' žizni i tvorčestvo L'va Nikolaeviča Tolstogo.* 1828–90. Moscow: GIXL, 1958; 1891–1910, Moscow: GIXL, 1960.

Hamburger, Käte. *Leo Tolstoi: Gestalt und Problem.* Bern: A. Francke, 1950.

Hansson, L. M. *We Women and Our Authors,* tr. H. Ramsden. London: John Lane, 1899.

Howells, W. D. *My Literary Passions.* New York: Harper and Brothers, 1895.

James, Henry. *The Future of the Novel.* New York: Vintage Books, 1956.

van Kaam, A. and Healy, K. *The Demon and the Dove.* Pittsburgh: Duquesne University Press, 1967.

Kuprejanova, E. "Vyraženie estetičestkyx vozzrenij i nravstvennyx iskanij L. Tolstogo v romane *Anna Karenina,*" *Russkaja literatura* III (1960).

L. N. Tolstoj v vospominanijax sovremennikov. Moscow, 1955.

Lavrin, Janko. *Tolstoy: An Approach.* New York: Macmillan, 1946.

Lawrence, D. H. *Reflections on the Death of a Porcupine and Other Essays.* Philadelphia: The Centaur Press, 1925.

Leavis, F. R. *Anna Karenina and Other Essays.* London: Chatto and Windus, 1967.

Mann, Thomas. *Goethe und Tolstoi.* Aachen: K. Spiertz, 1923.

Merejkowski, D. *Tolstoi as Man and Artist.* New York and London: G. P. Putnam and Sons, 1902.

Naumova, N. "Problema xaraktera v 'Vojne i mire,'" *Russkaja literatura* III (1960), 100–116.

Poggioli, Renato. *The Phoenix and the Spider.* Cambridge, Mass.: Harvard University Press, 1957.

Polner, T. *Lev Tolstoj i ego žena.* Paris: Sovremmenye zapiski, 1928.

Porché, F. *Portrait psychologique de Tolstoy.* Paris, 1935.

Posse, V. A. *Ljubov' v tvorčestve L'va Nikolaeviča Tolstogo.* 1917.

Rolland, Romain. *La vie de Tolstoi.* Paris: Hachette, 1922.

Rosen, N. "Chaos and Dostoevsky's Women," *Kenyon Review* XX (1958), 257–77.

Selivanova, N. N. *Russia's Women.* New York: E. P. Dutton and Co., 1923.

Šestov, L. *Dobro v učenii gr. Tolstogo i F. Nitše.* Berlin, 1923.

Šklovskij, V. *Lev Tolstoj.* Moscow: Molodaja Gvardija, 1963.

———. *Xod konja.* Berlin: Gelikon, 1923.

Spence, G. *Tolstoy the Ascetic.* New York, 1968.

Steiner, G. *Tolstoy or Dostoevsky.* New York: Knopf, 1959.

Stern, J. P. M. " 'Effi Brest': 'Madame Bovary': 'Anna Karenina,' " *Modern Language Review* LII, 1957.

Tolstoj, S. *Mat' i ded L. N. Tolstogo.* Moscow, 1928.

Trubicyn, N. *Obščestvennaja rol' ženščiny v izobraženii novejshej russkoj literatury.* Moscow: I. D. Cytin, 1907.

Williams, R. "Lawrence and Tolstoy," *Critical Quarterly* II (1960).

Ždanov, V. A. *Ljubov' v žizni L'va Tolstogo.* Moscow: M. & S. Sabašnikov, 1928.